The
Garland Library
of
War and Peace

The
Garland Library
of
War and Peace

Under the General Editorship of
Blanche Wiesen Cook, *John Jay College, C.U.N.Y.*
Sandi E. Cooper, *Richmond College, C.U.N.Y.*
Charles Chatfield, *Wittenberg University*

National Defence
A Study in Militarism

by
J. Ramsay MacDonald

with a new introduction
for the Garland Edition by
Catherine Ann Cline

Garland Publishing, Inc., New York & London
1972

Library of Congress Cataloging in Publication Data

MacDonald, James Ramsay, 1866-1937.
  National defence.

  (The Garland library of war and peace)
  Reprint of the 1917 ed.
  1. Militarism. 2. Great Britain--Defenses.
I. Title. II. Series.
UA10.M3 1972   355.02'13   70-147522
ISBN 0-8240-0310-1

Introduction

National Defence: A Study in Militarism *is of special interest because of its authorship. Ramsay MacDonald was later to serve seven years as prime minister of Great Britain, and for one year as foreign secretary. He thus provides the single case in modern history of a pacifist pamphleteer who, by attaining the highest position in the state, had the opportunity to implement the principles which he had preached. Were his earlier idealistic views jettisoned when he was faced with responsibility for dealing with the hard realities of the diplomatic scene, or did he remain faithful to his doctrines and, if so, what were the consequences for Britain's foreign policy? His career provides a rare opportunity to examine the question of whether a pacifist prime minister or president is a realistic possibility or a contradiction in terms.*

At the outbreak of World War I MacDonald, as the leader of the Labour party in the House of Commons, was a figure of some significance on the British political scene. It was a position to which he had risen from extremely inauspicious beginnings.[1] *Born in 1866 in Lossiemouth, a small Scottish fishing village, his childhood was characterized by utter poverty. Despite the penury of these years, his determined mother and the local schoolmaster, impressed with MacDonald's ability, enabled him to acquire somewhat more education than was usual for the village children. This was supplemented after his arrival in London at the age of twenty by wide reading. His educational background was therefore more extensive than that of most of the working class leaders of the Labour party with whom he was later to be associated.*

While earning a living first as secretary to a Liberal candidate for Parliament and later as a journalist, MacDonald became involved in the socialist revival of the 1880s. He was for a time a member of H. M. Hyndman's Social Democratic Federation (S. D. F.), the closest approximation to a Marxist group which Britain had produced. He then moved on to the Fabian Society. A sympathetic biographer explains that MacDonald's "scientific study made the narrow dogmatism of the one [the S. D. F.] impossible; [his] native temper was incompatible with the somewhat soulless opportunism and cut and dried collectivism of the other [the Fabians]." [2] Whatever the reason, MacDonald did not fit comfortably into these essentially middle-class groups, and the refusal of the Fabian Society to oppose the Boer War, which was the occasion of his resignation from the society, was only one of a series of disagreements which had arisen between him and the Fabian leadership. [3]

It was with the Independent Labour Party (I. L. P.), founded in 1893, that MacDonald was to

6

INTRODUCTION

become fully identified and which was to serve as his political base for the next thirty years. The I. L. P. was a working class socialist group dedicated to converting the workers to socialism of a vague but benevolent variety to be attained by democratic means.[4] One of its major aims was the establishment of a working class party, independent of both Liberals and Conservatives. An advance toward this goal was made in 1900 with the establishment of the Labour Representation Committee, an alliance of socialist groups and largely non-socialist trade unions, of which MacDonald became secretary. When in the election of 1906 twenty-nine candidates sponsored by the Committee, including MacDonald, were returned to Parliament, the Labour Representation Committee was transformed into the Labour party.

If the leading spirit of the Labour party in the prewar years was Keir Hardie, the Scottish miner, MacDonald was its strategist, tactician, and organizer. It was he who was responsible for the electoral pact with the Liberals which contributed to Labour's success in the election of 1906, and his grasp of parliamentary tactics led to his election as leader of the Parliamentary Labour party in 1911.

The British Labour party of the prewar years was largely indifferent to issues of foreign policy. The party's purpose was to protect the interests of the workers and the trade unions, and questions of foreign policy were regarded for the most part as distractions from its main business. Its status as a fourth party, with no possibility of forming a Government in the foreseeable future, made it unnecessary for its leaders to prepare themselves to undertake the responsibility of conducting foreign affairs. In any case, the majority of Labour M. P.'s were trade unionists who lacked the background of education and travel which might have stimulated concern for foreign policy issues. While the party was fond of passing resolutions in favor of peace and brotherhood, it lacked both interest and expertise in the field of foreign affairs.

MacDonald was one of the few exceptions to this general apathy within the Labour party in regard to foreign policy issues. Despite the fact that his official duties forced him to give prime consideration to domestic matters, he displayed zealous and informed interest in foreign affairs. He was the most persistent of the Labour M. P.'s in his attacks on the prewar foreign policy of Sir Edward Grey, the foreign secretary, centering his objections, as did some members of Grey's own Liberal party, on Britain's increasingly close ties with Czarist Russia. [5]

It is probable that MacDonald's growing concern with foreign policy was, in part, simply a matter of personal inclination. He did, however, enjoy the advantage of extensive travel denied to most members of the Labour party. His journeys were made possible by his marriage in 1896 to Margaret Ethel Gladstone, the daughter of a prominent scientist; the income which she received was sufficient to provide for leisure and the cost of travel.[6] *These trips — to India, South Africa, the United States, Canada, Australia, New Zealand, and, more frequently, to the Continent — appear to have been very purposeful expeditions. MacDonald sought out public officials, leaders of political parties, and socialists of various persuasions, thus acquiring an acquaintance with the internal politics of various countries as well as an insight into the views of leading politicians concerning the darkening international scene.*

Further contacts with socialist leaders on the Continent were provided by his attendance at the periodic congresses of the Second International, and the efforts of this organization to prevent the outbreak of war provide an important background for an understanding of the proposals set forth by MacDonald in National Defence. *From the founding meeting in 1889 the representatives of the European socialist parties sought consistently to formulate a strategy which would eliminate the fearful possibility that the workers of Europe might destroy one another in a general war.*[7] *They found no difficulty in analyzing the cause of war; it was capitalism which led inevitably to international conflict. Since capitalism was still the prevailing system, however, what socialists could do to halt these capitalist wars remained problematic. Though many radical solutions for action in the case of the outbreak of war were proposed — ranging from general strikes to armed insurrections by the workers against their own*

9

governments — national suspicions among the social-
ists themselves, fear of counter-action by the
belligerent governments, and a recognition of the
relative weakness of the socialist parties prevented the
adoption of any of these plans. More subtly, as public
education and the popular press expanded, workers
were drawn deeper into the prevailing mood of
nationalism and, on the Continent, even became
persuaded of the advantage of nationally oriented
economic policies. Thus, August 1914 found the
members of the Second International without a
determined course of anti-war action.

If the socialists of Europe failed to reach an accord
on coordinated action in the event of an actual
outbreak of war, they could more easily agree on
efforts to deprive their respective governments of the
means of waging war.[8] *Thus they committed them-*
selves to the campaign against "militarism," and they
sought by propaganda and by their votes in their
various parliaments to halt the increase in armaments
and, on the Continent, the extension of the period of
service under the conscription laws.

The major effort of the British Labour party in this
campaign was a special conference convened in
Leicester in January 1911 to consider the question of
armaments. The meeting was clearly designed to
exhort the workers to cultivate the right sentiments
on the question rather than to propose any concrete
solution.[9] *MacDonald presided, and his inspirational,*
if cloudy, platform style was perfectly suited to the

occasion.

> *In Leicester they had never indulged in the childish imagination of supposing that the security of a nation depended upon the number of Dreadnoughts that it put on the sea. They had never considered that a nation which based itself upon force and upon force only, could resist the antagonism of the other nations of the world. In Leicester they had always stood for the good old Biblical dictum which was going to survive this generation as it had survived many other generations, that righteousness alone exalteth a nation and provides for the permanent security and honor of a nation.* [10]

The increase in armaments, he continued, was a "policy that menaced our national existence." He concluded with characteristic fervor:

> *They were going to stretch their hands to their French comrades, . . . stretch their hands to their German comrades and all other comrades from the North Pole to the South, and from the rising to the setting sun, and they were going to proclaim that blessed day when the sword will be finally sheathed and when nations will pursue the ways of peace and follow the arts of war no more.* [11]

The delegates dutifully voted unanimously for a resolution urging that disputes between nations be settled "not by brute force but by reason and arbitration," and urging British workers to cooperate with their counterparts in other nations to secure international peace. [12] *The conference adjourned, and the arms race continued; the rhetoric of the British section of the Second International had no discernible effect on the policy of the British government.*

With the outbreak of World War I in August 1914 the ineffectiveness of the Second International's twenty-five-year-long effort to mobilize the working classes of Europe against war rapidly became apparent. The workers, with few exceptions, rallied to their respective national causes. The British Labour party officially supported Britain's participation in the conflict and, from 1915 to the end of the war, participated in the coalition governments responsible for its direction.

Ramsay MacDonald's conduct in this crisis suggests that, however vague his concept of internationalism, it was deeply and sincerely held. On August 3, after Grey's masterly exposition in the House of Commons of the case for British intervention in the war, MacDonald spoke in opposition, arguing that British security was not at stake, and that a European holocaust was hardly necessary to defend the neutrality of Belgium.[13] When, on August 5, with the war fever mounting, the Labour M. P.'s refused to endorse MacDonald's reading in the House of Commons of a resolution critical of Grey's diplomacy, he resigned his chairmanship of the Parliamentary Labour party. Whatever brave prophecies MacDonald might make about the ultimate vindication of his position by the opinion of posterity,[14] he was

12

clearly, at the moment, moving rapidly into the political wilderness.

Since MacDonald's opposition to the war severely reduced his effectiveness in the House of Commons, a large part of his energies was devoted during the war years to the propaganda activities of "pacifist" groups which shared his views. The I. L. P., in which he had long been a major figure, remained staunchly true to the ideals of the Second International, and, at the cost of a large loss of membership,[15] denounced the "capitalist" war.[16] Since the I. L. P., despite its disagreement with the Labour party on the issue of the war, remained affiliated with the larger organization, MacDonald and his anti-war colleagues retained a precarious foothold in the Labour movement, and they were thus in a position to recover their influence quickly when Labour's earlier enthusiastic support of the war began to wane in the closing months of 1917.

In addition to his activity in the I. L. P., Mac-Donald played an important role in the Union of Democratic Control (U.D.C.), a group organized on the outbreak of the war to work for the elimination of "secret diplomacy," which its members regarded as the cause of the war, and to plan for a just peace based on a "new diplomacy," reflecting the will of the benevolent and peace-loving "peoples." Of the five founders of the U. D. C., four were middle-class Liberals who had been severe critics of Britain's prewar foreign policy. MacDonald alone had ties with a working-class organization, albeit the numerically weak I. L. P. With MacDonald providing the link, cooperation between the two groups was soon close.[17]

MacDonald's National Defence, which first appeared in January 1917, was one of the numerous pamphlets produced by these energetic but beleaguered anti-war organizations in order to win support for their highly unpopular position. As a hastily written piece of propaganda it should perhaps not be judged too harshly. There is no denying the fact, however, that its defects are characteristic of virtually every speech, book, and pamphlet produced by the man who was to dominate the British Labour party in the 1920s. Even the most superficial reading reveals blatant contradictions. On page 84 MacDonald remarks gloomily, and with some prescience:

> *I see no prospect of a final solution of Balkan difficulties; I see no chance of a satisfactory settlement of Poland. . . . A democratic Germany will, indeed, have no difficulty in finding many opportunities in the next generation to challenge the decision of this war and to write a sequel to it more congenial to the German spirit than the record that is now being made.*

By page 130 he is, however, much more cheerful.

> *As to programmes [for peace settlement] I do not believe they present much difficulty provided they are considered by the peoples themselves. The restoration of Belgium, the rehabilitation of France, the settlement of*

INTRODUCTION

> the Balkans, the re-establishment of a Polish autonomy,
> outlets for Germany — these and kindred questions are
> so agreed upon really in the hearts of the people that no
> Conference representative of the people could fail to
> settle them, or could quarrel about the principles upon
> which they ought to be settled....

The prose is cloudy and vague. At what appears to be
the climax of the book he announces that

> The days of peace picnics and polite and meaningless
> speeches are over. They have been empty. Energy that is
> sleepless and a policy which is pursued from day to day
> and with complete detail, watching every move in the
> diplomatic game and with a thoroughly efficient Intelli-
> gence Department and Parliamentary policy, are now
> required.... (p. 120)

The reader is eager to be told, by the man who
presided over one of the better attended "peace
picnics" of the prewar years, the concrete details of
this more realistic policy. The author, however,
moves on to other matters. It is a temptation to
believe that Ramsay MacDonald had, in fact, no
program to offer beyond a fuzzy idealism.

A careful examination of National Defence
suggests, however, that MacDonald did indeed have a
specific proposal in mind. In circuitous fashion he
urges a revival of the prewar efforts of the Second
International to organize and coordinate anti-war
opinion across national boundaries. Democratic or-

15

ganizations in various countries, he suggests, should consult regularly and "should confer simultaneously with the official diplomatists and, free from old traditions and modes of diplomacy, should agree among themselves about an international action which will be cooperative and express the really pacific national wills" (p. 16). In another effort to express the same idea he explains:

> *A strong united effort will be required in which enlightened opinion in the various nations must be in the very closest communion, must act both officially and unofficially on arranged plans in the separate States, must devise and support policies to strengthen the pacific movement in each country, and must create both a national and international political organization which, in every country will act in unity. (p. 120)*

When the official diplomacy of a nation acts in opposition to this "machinery of democratic diplomacy," a general strike should be called by the cooperating groups (p. 17).

If MacDonald was, as he appears to be, recommending a return to the course attempted by the Second International, why did he not say so? Probably his contacts with the middle-class members of the U.D.C. had made him aware of the resources of pacifist sentiment in groups outside the working class, and he was here suggesting a broader effort which would involve international contacts among groups other than the socialists.

INTRODUCTION

A more important reason for his reticence in indicating that he was, in essence, proposing a revival of the efforts of the Second International was doubtless the fact that the anti-war efforts of that group had proven to be totally ineffective. He alludes, however, to its disappointing record and finds an excuse for its inability to implement its ideals.

The International Socialist movement bade fair to begin the new order, but the war came too soon for it. It had not established its grip firmly enough. . . . (p. 16)

MacDonald's argument that the International's quarter century of fruitless effort to work out an effective anti-war policy among the workers of Europe fell short of success only because of lack of time suggests the touching, if uncritical, loyalty to the ideals of this organization which he was to display in the years ahead.

The other major points developed by MacDonald in National Defence *require less tortuous exegesis. He favored an early peace which would, by its moderation, encourage pacific behavior in the future on the part of the enemy. Arguing that the political goal of the Allies was not only a democratic Germany, but a democratic Germany whose public would accept the peace terms "with no hot feelings in its heart" (p. 88), he expressed the view that the moment for such a settlement was more propitious at the beginning of 1917 than it would be after prolonged fighting had*

17

brought about that nation's military collapse.

> *I believe that the people of Germany now, if released from the strain of war and the necessity of presenting a united front to the enemy, would end the dominance of militarism, would remove its menace from Europe, and would enter into the cooperation of States which will have to be established if Europe is to be saved from destruction, and I further believe they will be less inclined to do this after another year of war. (p. 129)*

In MacDonald's view it was not Germany alone but all nations which must be freed from the curse of "militarism," and it is on this point that he places his greatest emphasis. Ignoring the orthodox socialist explanation that wars are the result of capitalism (which it is doubtful that he ever accepted), and placing rather less emphasis on "secret diplomacy" as the cause of war than his middle-class allies of the U.D.C., he points to militarism as the source of conflict. He asserts that World War I came about "because preparations for war and a military policy of defence must always issue in war and provide a reason for war" (p. 44). In his view, ". . . so long as there are armies there will be wars" (p. 14). He maintains that armaments not only provide no safety, they weaken the security of a nation by encouraging its neighbors to arm in turn. The distinction between offensive and defensive weapons is, in his opinion, meaningless (p. 39). If peace is to be achieved, nations must disarm, and no arguments on grounds of *security or the maintenance of peace through strength can be permitted to justify deviation from this policy.*

It is this uncompromising view concerning the necessity of disarmament which leads to MacDonald's rather surprising attack on the proposals of the League to Enforce Peace, an American group which included prominent figures such as former President Taft. Like other organizations in Britain and America which had devoted themselves to the problem of devising machinery to ensure that World War I should not be repeated, the group was working to build public support for the establishment of an international peace-keeping organization after the war. They were thus the allies of the U. D. C. which had from its foundation included the formation of an "International Council" among its major goals. The program of the American group, however, placed special emphasis on provisions for economic and forcible sanctions against aggressors, a point on which the schemes of the various internationalist groups differed.[18] Dismissing economic sanctions as useless (pp. 113-4), MacDonald concentrates his attack on the recommendations for the use of collective force. "The [proposed] League to Enforce Peace," he charged, ". . . contains in itself all the evils of militarism" (p. 59). These proposals would perpetuate the idea that armies are necessary for security. Such an organization might well become a new Holy Alliance, suppressing freedom in the

19

interests of existing governments. MacDonald was convinced that "any machinery controlling military power can be captured by war-making interests and instincts. . . . the problem of defence is not how to protect ourselves by force against enmity, but how to remove enmity" (p. 63). Except for the vague references to the "machinery of democratic diplomacy" noted above, the knotty problem of the means by which enmities might be removed is not pursued.

During the years from 1918 to 1922 MacDonald demonstrated again, as he had at the outbreak of the war, that his vacuous rhetoric did not signify lack of commitment to his ideals. Involuntarily freed from parliamentary duties by his defeat in the election of 1918, he worked devotedly for the reestablishment of his cherished Second International. The bitter mutual recriminations among the socialists of the former belligerents proved far less difficult to surmount than the split in the movement occasioned by the Bolshevik Revolution in Russia and the establishment of the Third International dominated by Moscow.[19] When his own Independent Labour Party disaffiliated from the older organization, he opposed the move and continued in his capacity as a secretary of the Second International.[20] During his time-consuming negotiations with the Second-and-a-half International in Vienna and his trip to Russia as a representative of the Second International to investigate the treatment of Social Democrats in Georgia by the Communists [21] he remained firmly wedded to his prewar

20

INTRODUCTION

vision — an international organization of democratic socialist parties which would provide a bulwark against war. The unity of European socialism was shattered beyond repair, however, and the most important outcome of his efforts was the discrediting of the Communist party in Britain itself. At this time MacDonald doubtless entertained ambitions for the revival of his career in British politics, which makes his gallant expenditure of energy on behalf of the increasingly hopeless cause of the Second International all the more impressive.[22]

MacDonald's return to the House of Commons in 1922 and his subsequent election to the chairmanship of the Parliamentary Labour party represented more than a resumption of the position that he had held in 1914. The size of the Labour party had greatly increased, and its interests had broadened. From the fourth party of prewar years it had become the official Opposition, and a Labour Government now seemed within the realm of possibility. MacDonald's concern with foreign policy which had been exceptional among Labourites before 1914 was now characteristic of large segments of the party. The middle-class recruits who had streamed into the party after the war were motivated in large part by their disillusionment with both the war and the peace for which they held the older parties responsible.[23] *The workers had been jolted by the war into a recognition of the effect of foreign policy decisions on their lives. MacDonald had returned to the leadership of a party*

*which might soon become responsible for the con-
duct of foreign affairs, and whose membership was
likely to prove both informed and demanding in this
area.*

*The first Labour Government, in which MacDonald
served as both prime minister and foreign secretary,
came to office in 1924. While its record in domestic
affairs was unimpressive — no worse, and certainly no
better, than that of other Governments of the
interwar years — it was widely regarded at the time as
having achieved substantial success in the area of
foreign policy.*[24] *These accomplishments, which
appear somewhat less imposing in the light of later
developments, were in complete harmony with the
policies and principles MacDonald had espoused in
National Defence.*

*The Labour Government's reputation for success in
foreign affairs rested to a great extent on its handling
of the "German problem." MacDonald sought pains-
takingly for the kind of settlement which he had
described in 1917 — one which public opinion in
Germany could accept "with no hot feelings in its
heart." It seemed evident that the Treaty of Versailles
had failed in that respect, and his prediction that a
democratic Germany would prove no less resentful of
a harsh peace than an authoritarian regime seemed
borne out in the months before he took office by the
Weimar Republic's refusal to make reparations payments — a default which led to the French occupation of the Ruhr. Although MacDonald took charge*

INTRODUCTION

of Britain's foreign policy at a time of serious tension on the Continent, it was likewise a moment which presented certain opportunities for a settlement, and he exploited these favorable circumstances to the fullest. Germany had become weary of the economic cost of her policy of passive resistance in the Ruhr, and the French were becoming aware of the futility of the occupation. The advent of leaders more conciliatory than their predecessors — Stresemann in Germany and Herriot in France — increased the prospect of finding an accommodation. The report of the Dawes Committee, a group of experts appointed at the urging of Lord Curzon, MacDonald's predecessor as foreign secretary,[25] provided proposals which could serve as the basis of negotiations. At MacDonald's invitation, representatives of the former Allied governments met in London for over a month; in the final weeks they were joined by German delegates. Out of these meetings, over which Mac-Donald presided with great skill and tact, came the agreement known as the Dawes Plan: the evacuation of the Ruhr by France in return for Germany's agreement to an arrangement which left the total of reparations intact, but reduced the annual payments. Tensions harmful to both the political and economic stability of Europe had been reduced, and the first step toward the revision of the Treaty of Versailles had been achieved peacefully.

In his policy toward the League of Nations MacDonald adherred strictly to the principles which he had laid down in National Defence. *He favored an international organization, but he opposed sanctions. The League should work for a system of arbitration and an agreement on disarmament rather than concerning itself with the organization of collective force. On taking office he was presented with the Draft Treaty of Mutual Assistance, a proposal submitted to the various governments by the Fourth Assembly of the League. The Treaty was an effort to strengthen the rather vague provisions in the League Covenant for cooperative action against an aggressor by strengthening the executive powers of the League and providing for regional defensive pacts. While paying tribute to the sincerity of those who had produced the proposal, MacDonald rejected it as "essentially a war preparation document."* [26]

If it seems curious, in the light of this action, that the Labour party acquired a reputation as a proponent of collective security, the explanation lies in the action of the Labour Government's representatives at the Fifth Assembly of the League. Determined to extend the arbitration provisions of the Covenant and to bring about general disarmament, they found that French acceptance of their proposals could be gained only by strengthening sanctions as well. They therefore consented reluctantly to the inclusion of provisions for military sanctions in what became known as the Geneva Protocol. This was the price that they paid for the extension of the arbitration requirements of the

League and the condition that the protocol would come into effect only after the conclusion of a successful disarmament conference. The Labour Government fell before the Geneva Protocol could be ratified. Although it is doubtful that the Labour Cabinet would have agreed to the plan without some modifications,[27] it remained the official policy of the party. Virtually no one in the Labour party, least of all its leader, showed any enthusiasm for the agreement to use collective force against an aggressor. Employing one of the biological similes of which he was fond, MacDonald expressed the hope that the sanctions provisions of the protocol

> . . . will remain in it like the atrophied remnants that our own bodies bear of the creatures of lower [status] through which the line of our physiological ancestry runs.[28]

On another occasion he admitted:

> I never have regarded these powers as being of any importance except insofar as their presence on paper is a harmless drug to soothe the nerves.[29]

In short, the arbitration and disarmament features of the protocol would make it unnecessary ever to resort to sanctions. Presiding over an army and a navy had not altered MacDonald's view that disarmament was the only road to peace.

INTRODUCTION

The second Labour Government from 1929 to 1931 was in many ways a repetition of the first. Once again it was unable to cope with domestic problems, its failures in this area leading finally to the financial and political crisis of 1931. Its conduct of foreign policy appeared, in contrast, to be attended with considerable success. As in 1924 its policies were designed to conciliate Germany and to advance disarmament and enlarge the machinery of arbitration. The acceptance of the Young Plan, which further reduced the German reparations burden, and the agreement to withdraw occupation forces from the Rhineland in 1930, five years in advance of the date set in the Treaty of Versailles, were victories for revisionism. The Labour Government fulfilled its pledge to sign the Optional Clause and the General Act, thus committing Britain to submit both justiciable and non-justiciable disputes to arbitration. The London Naval Conference of 1930 extended the scope of the naval limitations agreements of the Washington Conference of 1922 among the three major naval powers, Britain, the United States, and Japan. There appeared to be hopeful developments even on the thorny issue of military disarmament, and the long-delayed Disarmament Conference was scheduled to meet in February 1932.[30]

Since MacDonald confined himself to the post of prime minister in the second Labour Government, a great share of the responsibility for the working out of these policies lay with the foreign secretary,

26

Arthur Henderson. MacDonald's continuing interest in foreign affairs meant, however, that the foreign secretary was by no means allowed a free hand. The prime minister firmly vetoed various tentative efforts by Henderson and Lord Cecil, the British delegate at the League of Nations, to allay French fears and thus to hasten the process of revision and disarmament by strengthening provisions for sanctions in case of aggression. Ironically, support for MacDonald's opposition to collective security, which sprang from his long-standing aversion to "militarism," came from military and naval advisers who argued against any extension of Britain's commitments.[31]

An assessment of MacDonald's impact on foreign policy should be based on his record in the two Labour governments of the 1920s rather than on his period as prime minister of the National Government from 1931 to 1935. In the earlier decade he was at the height of his powers, and his commanding position in his party gave his foreign policy efforts a strong domestic political base. Having broken with the Labour party in 1931, he was personally without party support while leader of a Coalition Government dependent on Conservative votes. His political weakness combined with failing health made him increasingly a figurehead as the real power passed to Stanley Baldwin, leader of the Conservative party.

If MacDonald's role in these years was of relatively minor importance in terms of British foreign policy, the views he expressed provide a melancholy com-

ment on the fate of a pacifist politician in the 1930s. When Germany left the Disarmament Conference, withdrew from the League of Nations, and began arming, more or less openly, in defiance of the provisions of the Treaty of Versailles, MacDonald was forced to reconsider his cherished beliefs. The issuing of the famous White Paper, Statement Relating to Defense,[32] *calling for British rearmament was the final important act of his political career. In his defense of the White Paper*[33] *he observed sadly that no single nation could afford unilaterally to remain unarmed and that the low level of Britain's military forces was a threat to peace. In contrast to his earlier view that no distinction could be made between an offensive and defensive military establishment, he pleaded for "defence armaments." The rhetorical habits of a lifetime remained, however. In a pathetic echo of* National Defence *he solemnly warned the British public against being "drawn into the whirlpool of militarism." "It has been abundantly proved," he repeated once again, "that a heavily armed nation does not frighten other possible war makers to pursue the ways of peace." He urged the nation to entertain "no delusion as to the very limited security which can be provided by arms," and to resist the view "that war preparations either by alliances or military expenditure are ultimate securities that peace may be kept." Having made his ritual denunciation of militarism, he proceeded to warn against what was a more real danger in the Britain of 1934, "a peace panic [which] in an armed world ... is as certain as a war panic to produce war."* This was a clear reference to the by-election in East Fulham, normally a Conservative stronghold, in which the Conservative candidate, who strongly advocated rearmament, had been defeated by a Labourite, well indoctrinated by Ramsay MacDonald, who argued that there was "no security in armaments." [34]

MacDonald may be forgiven these somewhat contradictory remarks; the events on the international scene in the 1930s created confusion in many minds. It is hardly surprising that the man who had worked so devotedly for disarmament and for generous treatment for Germany should have displayed some ambiguity as he abandoned his long-established beliefs. It is less MacDonald's inconsistency in the 1930s than his rigid consistency in earlier years which has led to criticism. Had he been less "soft" on Germany, had he agreed to putting some teeth into the League Covenant, might not the story of the 1930s have been different? Such a view is based on the dubious assumptions either that a harsher policy toward Germany on the part of the Western powers would somehow have prevented Hitler's rise to power, or that the governments of France and Britain would have accorded to League provisions for forcible sanctions a respect they did not display during the Rhineland crisis for the much more specific commitments undertaken in the Locarno Pact. [35] While MacDonald's policy was an ultimate failure, it is *difficult to demonstrate that any other course of action had a greater chance of success. Neither pacifists nor their critics can draw any support for their positions from the career of Ramsay Mac-Donald. His principles proved no cure for the international problems of the 1920s; there is no evidence that the effort to apply them made matters any worse.*

Catherine Ann Cline
Department of History
Catholic University of America

INTRODUCTION

NOTES

[1] *There is at present no satisfactory biography of MacDonald. L. MacNeil Weir's* The Tragedy of Ramsay MacDonald *(London, 1938) is a polemic against MacDonald; H. Hessell Tiltman,* J. Ramsay MacDonald: Labour's Man of Destiny *(New York, 1929) is adulatory; Iconoclast [Mary Agnes Hamilton],* J. Ramsay MacDonald: The Man of Tomorrow *(New York, 1924), although written when the author was clearly under MacDonald's spell, contains some perceptive comments. Lord Elton's* The Life of James Ramsay MacDonald *(London, 1939), while the best study available, lacks detachment, since Elton was one of the few Labourites to support MacDonald's formation of a Coalition Government in 1931. Benjamin Sacks,* J. Ramsay MacDonald in Thought and Action *(Albuquerque, New Mexico, 1952) provides a useful summary of MacDonald's views on major issues. A biography by Mr. David Marquand, M. P., is expected to be published shortly.*

[2] *Iconoclast, op cit., p. 66.*

[3] *On the friction between MacDonald and the leaders of the Fabian Society see Beatrice Webb,* Our Partnership *(New York, 1948), pp. 132, 188, 192-3, 229-30, 260-1, 271, 276, and A. M. McBriar,* Fabian Socialism & English Politics, 1884-1918 *(Cambridge, 1962), pp. 120, 124, 219, 291-4, 303-4.*

[4] *For a brief history of the I. L. P. see Robert E. Dowse,* Left in the Center: The Independent Labour Party, 1893-1940 *(Evanston, Ill., 1966).*

[5] *On the criticism of Grey's policy see John A. Murray, "Foreign Policy Debated: Sir Edward Grey and His Critics,"* Power, Public Opinion and Diplomacy, *eds. Lillian Parker Wallace and William C. Askew (Durham, N.C., 1959), pp. 140-71. Another major exception to the indifference to foreign policy among Labourites was Keir Hardie who led the opposition to Edward VII's meeting with the Czar in 1908.*

[6] *His wife's contribution to MacDonald's career went far beyond providing economic security. She was a serious and informed social reformer who was regarded as an expert on the problem of women employed in "sweated" industries. See Elie Halévy,* History of the English People: Epilogue *(2nd rev. ed.; London, 1952), Book I, pp.*

NOTES

248-52; Book II, p. 510. Her early death in 1911 was regarded by both friend and foe as crucial in explaining the development of MacDonald's personality in later years. To his admirers it made him a tragic, and therefore glamorous, figure. For his critics, the absence of her influence helped to explain what they regarded as the deepening defects in his character. See Tiltman, op. cit., pp. 91-5 and Mary Agnes Hamilton's sketch of MacDonald, written after his break with the Labour party in 1931, Remembering My Good Friends (London, 1944), pp. 120-30. For MacDonald's tribute to his wife see his memoir Margaret Ethel MacDonald (London, 1912).

[7] For the Second International in this period see Julius Braunthal, History of the International, 1864-1914 (London, 1966), trans. Henry Collins and Kenneth Mitchell, pp. 325-54.

[8] Ibid., pp. 328-34. Attempts to halt the arms race were, of course, not limited to the socialists, but extended from the Czar to various pacifist groups. For the early years of the twentieth century see Merze Tate, The Disarmament Illusion: The Movement for a Limitation of Armaments to 1907 (New York, 1942). A brief survey of these efforts to 1914 is provided in the introductory chapter of Gerda Richards Crosby, Disarmament and Peace in British Politics (Cambridge, Mass., 1957).

[9] "Report of Special Conference on Disarmament and the International Situation, January 31, 1911," is included in Report of the Eleventh Annual Conference of the Labour Party (February, 1911). The only proposal for specific action, an amendment by Keir Hardie authorizing the opening of discussions with socialist parties on the Continent to examine the question of the use of the general strike in the event of the outbreak of war, was defeated. See pp. 116-9.

[10] Ibid., p. 111.

[11] Ibid., p. 113.

[12] Loc. cit.

[13] House of Commons Debates, Vol. 65, Fifth Series, 1821-3.

[14] Ibid., 1823.

[15] Beatrice Webb's Diaries: 1912-1924, ed. Margaret I. Cole (London, 1952), p. 34 (Entry for May 3, 1915).

[16] See the I. L. P. newspaper, Labour Leader, August 6, 1914.

[17] For a full study of the U. D. C. during the war see Marvin Swartz, The Union of Democratic Control in British Politics during the First

NOTES

World War *(Oxford, 1971). The wartime cooperation between middle-class pacifists and anti-war socialists was to have significant consequences: an effective agitation in favor of moderate war aims was maintained throughout the war, the Labour party, increasingly weary of the carnage and suspicious of the motives of Britain's leaders in continuing the war, enlisted in the crusade against the "old diplomacy," and many prominent middle-class Liberals, impressed with Labour's support of the "new diplomacy," were attracted to membership in the Labour party, hitherto an exclusively working-class organization.*

[18] *For a comparison of the programs of the various internationalist groups in Britain see* Catherine Ann Cline, Recruits to Labour: The British Labour Party, 1914-1931 *(Syracuse, N.Y., 1963), pp. 15-7.*

[19] *See* Julius Braunthal, History of the International, 1914-1943 *(London, 1967), trans. John Clark, pp. 149-254.*

[20] Richard W. Lyman, *"James Ramsay MacDonald and the Leadership of the Labour Party,"* Journal of British History, *II (November, 1962), 144-5.*

[21] *For MacDonald's activities in the Second International at this time see* Braunthal, History of the International, 1914-1943, *pp. 161, 242, 246, 248-9.*

[22] *MacDonald's preoccupation with the affairs of the Second International is used as evidence that he was not at this time "pursuing with single-minded determination the leadership of the [Labour] party" in* Lyman, op. cit., *p. 141.*

[23] *For this group see* Cline, op. cit., *Chapters I and IV.*

[24] *For a full study of the 1924 Labour Government see* Richard W. Lyman, The First Labour Government, 1924 *(London, 1957).*

[25] *Curzon's initiative reflects the fact that the Conservatives were by this time as eager as the Labour party to reduce the reparations burden on Germany. See* Charles Loch Mowat, Britain between the Wars *(Boston, 1971), pp. 157-60.*

[26] Report of the Twenty-Fourth Annual Conference of the Labour Party *(October, 1924), p. 108.*

[27] *For the evidence on this point see* Cline, op. cit., *pp. 92-3. For another view see* Mowat, op. cit., *p. 181.*

[28] *As quoted in* Sacks, op. cit., *p. 557.*

[29] J. Ramsay MacDonald, *"Protocol and Pact,"* Labour Magazine, *III (April, 1925), p. 532.*

NOTES

[30] On the foreign policy of the second Labour Government see Henry R. Winkler, "Arthur Henderson," The Diplomats, 1919-1939, eds. Gordon Craig and Felix Gilbert (Princeton, N.J., 1953), pp. 311-43, and David Carlton, MacDonald versus Henderson (New York, 1970).

[31] Carlton, op. cit., pp. 28-9, 87-90, 129-32.

[32] Statement Relating to Defense (Cmd. 4827; 1935).

[33] MacDonald's position is presented by him in "Peace and Defence," News-Letter V-VI (December 22, 1934), 100-2; "Peace, Germany and Stresa," News-Letter, VII-VIII (April 27, 1935), 38-40; "Peace and Defence II," News-Letter, V-VI (March 16, 1935), 204-5.

[34] A. J. P. Taylor suggests that the reason for the Conservative defeat was dissatisfaction with domestic policy rather than the issue of rearmament. He recognizes, however, that the Government interpreted it as evidence of strong pacifist sentiment. Baldwin described the election as "a nightmare," English History, 1914-1945 (Oxford, 1965), p. 367, and concluded that any hope of strengthening the armed forces had been lost "in a wild flood of pacifism." Margaret George, The Warped Vision (Pittsburgh, Pa. 1965), p. 43.

[35] The Treaty of Locarno was a multi-lateral agreement among France, Britain, Germany, and Italy to guarantee the eastern frontier of France. It was concluded by the Conservative Government in 1925.

NATIONAL DEFENCE

NATIONAL DEFENCE

A STUDY IN MILITARISM

BY

J. RAMSAY MACDONALD, M.P.

LONDON: GEORGE ALLEN & UNWIN LTD.

RUSKIN HOUSE   40 MUSEUM STREET, W.C. 1

First edition published January 1917
Reprinted March   .   . 1917

TO

THE TRADE UNIONISTS OF THE COUNTRY

WHO ARE AT THE PARTING OF THE WAYS, AND

UPON WHOSE COURAGE AND WISDOM

THE FUTURE OF EUROPE SO

LARGELY DEPENDS

CONTENTS

INTRODUCTION

I HAVE tried in this book to prove that militarism of an unlimited kind is a necessary consequence of the political policy which European States have been pursuing hitherto. For some years I have been forced against my will nearer and nearer to the conclusion that, given the way in which we have been conducting our foreign affairs and the features which our *entente* with Russia and France have been assuming, war was becoming inevitable [1] and the policy of the National Service League was becoming an unavoidable calamity. We could not get the country to take a sufficiently apprehensive interest in its European policy, and the others could not induce it to face the responsibilities of its position.[2] It was right in refusing militarism, and

---

[1] Whoever has had an opportunity of reading the dispatches of the Belgian Ministers in London, Paris, and Berlin, published in America in 1915, under the title of *European Politics during the Decade before the War as described by Belgian Diplomatists*, will understand how this inevitability was troubling the minds of those who were well informed, and how the inevitability arose. The point is also dealt with by Mr. Lowes Dickinson in his *The European Anarchy*, George Allen & Unwin, 2s. 6d. net. See also Mr. Morel's *Truth and the War*, 2s.

[2] But note the argument in Chapter IV.

yet it would not take the trouble to avoid war. That was the dilemma in which we were.

When the war broke out conscription could not be avoided. We had committed ourselves to policies and expeditions which made every other method of raising the necessary troops a mere makeshift. If voluntaryism could have been saved, it was not by recruiting meetings which only hastened it to its end, but by a policy which at the outset would have defined in severely precise language our responsibilities and our purpose in entering the war, and which would have kept open channels for diplomatic negotiation. That was never done except in perorations which increased fervour and misunderstanding at the same time. When the Coalition was formed, voluntaryism, doomed for months, actually died, because the Cabinet had to be kept together, and in the face of the military demands the conscriptionists had to be appeased. Labour in particular lost its chance of saving the nation by keeping control upon militarism, and the country set out upon the road to military victory through the ruin of civil liberty. We sacrificed the future to the present when we might have saved both. In this book I deal with the future.

Those who read what I have written will have two questions constantly in their minds, and I will deal with them straight away. The first is, " Would you disarm immediately after the war, whether other

nations did so or not?" and the second is, "How
is the old order of policy which you say brought
the war upon Europe to be ended?"

It is impossible to disarm right away. When
one has been pursuing for a long time a wrong
path, one has to consume some little time in returning to wiser ways. There must be an intervening
time, the features of which (for instance, how armaments can be progressively reduced) require for
their discussion a book to itself. I wish to raise
issues more fundamental and controlling than expediencies, because I feel that nothing will injure
the future more than if we accept expediencies as
final settlements—than if we assume that the best
we can do for the moment is to be regarded as
satisfactory. It must be remembered that there
will be no war for at least ten or twenty years
after this, and we have that time in which to lay the
foundations of peace. What I insist upon is that
if during these years false starts are made or un-
stable securities accepted, the next generation will
find itself in our position. There is no compromise
possible in militarism. It is all or none.

I do not discuss temporary expediencies and
makeshifts. I have tried to bring my readers face
to face with ultimate and governing facts. The
important thing is definitely to see one's error,
definitely to understand it, definitely to turn one's
back upon it. And it is particularly important as

regards militarism to see that every—even the best —halfway house is a dangerous dwelling-place, and that so long as militarism in any shape or form exists it is a menace to peace.

This country has been grievously misled by a kind of pious pacifism, which lulled it into a false sense of security, which refused to face the truth, which allowed it to drift into war whilst it was preaching peace, and which, when the war broke out, chirped about this being the last of the wars and linked its arms in those of Mars as the saviour of society and the herald of peace. This kind of pacifism is to be in the future as impotent for good and as fruitful of evil as it has been in the past.

There can be no peace until the people search for it with two assumptions in their minds : the first, that war is not made by a conscious effort of any one's will, but is an event in political policy, an impasse; the second, that arms never can provide for national security, that they only keep nations insecure, and that they evolve an organization, a morality, a necessity, and an expediency based upon Force as Right, and that these are constantly extending their authority and their threats against liberty and self-government.

Militarism has increased its power enormously within the last century, not because it has been successful but because it has failed. The nations have increased their military preparations and handed themselves over to military control, obedient to exactly the same impulse as that which urges a gambler to increase his stakes. When a gambler working upon a system loses, he increases his risks till he loses all. After every war the failure of militarism to secure the purposes of the war and remove the causes of war has led to demands for a more efficient and thorough militarism. I might vary the simile. The nations have been like sick men taking patent medicines. The less good the trusted specific does, the bigger the dose they take. When nations fear each other, Governments have an unlimited command over their resources and their capacity to sacrifice. To organize the power of resistance and attack seems such an obvious security to those who do not think of consequences, and armies seem so necessary, that no cautious man can question them if he does not follow cause and effect far enough. The truth which I want to drive home is that the nation which trusts to the sword must perish by the sword, because it has committed itself to a system of defence which cannot defend but which must in the end destroy.

I have no belief that the waste and cruelties of war will ever end it. If that were so, the mere development of the powers of destruction would drive nations to seek peace. War belongs to emotions more primitive and elusive than those

which determine bargains over a counter. Its very
sacrifices are acceptable to people like martyrdom.
We say truly that armaments and war depend on
political policy, but that is only part of the truth.
Armaments and armies also influence political
policy. We live in a world of action and reaction, of causes producing effects, and effects
becoming causes for further effects. I believe that
so long as there are armies there will be wars,
because the existence of armies produces those situa-
tions under which the sacrifices of war become
acceptable to the people. That is the fact which
rules everything, and if we do not face it we face
nothing.

I therefore say that whatever the intermediate
stage may be, it must be tolerated only as an
intermediate stage in which there should be no
lingering, and that the people all the time should
be working and agreeing to hurry through with
it and so get to the end of it.

Then, as to the second question. The existing
order of policy and tradition cannot make peace.
In its hands this war will just leave behind it
the usual crop of unsolved problems and irrita-
tions which in due course will strengthen militarism and diplomacy. Then Europe will steadily
drift into another conflict. If this war has not
forfeited the confidence of the masses of Europe
in the kind of Governments which they have been

having, there is to be no guarantee of peace in
Europe. International relations are controlled in
such a way as to make war inevitable. To discuss
the consequences of this would require a book, but
the fundamental points of the programme of the
Union of Democratic Control and its publications
may be consulted.

To think of peace under such conditions is like
expecting a warm, gentle, nourishing rain when
the temperature is below zero. It is therefore
futile to think of ending militarism and war
under existing diplomatic conditions. The one
depends upon the other ; both must be destroyed
together. This war is the proof of the failure
of both.

Special as may be the German responsibility
to-day, no greater misfortune could befall Europe
than if that responsibility were made to obscure
those of a more general character. If the wider
truth is not seen, Europe will be left in the clutches
of militarism. That is why so many interests are
anxious to make people believe that one man made
the war or that one national clique forced it. The
one man's head may be chopped off, the national
clique may be deprived of power—but the armies
will remain. If the victimized nations could but
see that this fraud of force to which they are
trusting is the very thing which is oppressing them
and scourging them, if they once grasp that the

old order of diplomacy and militarism has made
the war inevitable and will continue to make war
inevitable, then that old order will disappear and
war will go with it.

My answer to the second question therefore is,
that so soon as peace appears above the horizon
the democratic organizations of the various nations
(Labour in particular) should get together, should
confer simultaneously with the official diplomatists,
and, free from old traditions and modes of diplomacy, should agree amongst themselves about an
international action which will be co-operative and
express the really pacific national wills.

In one of the means for securing national unity
I am particularly interested. The International
Socialist movement bade fair to begin the new
order, but the war came too soon for it. It had
not established its grip firmly enough, and the
current down the rapids sped too swiftly since
the Agadir incident for any international unofficial
movement to withstand it and save Europe from
having to tumble over the waterfall. Still, we
must return to the corporate action of the workers
of Europe. The working classes must build up
a Labour international diplomacy (other political
and social sections doing their share in ways suit-
able to themselves), which will be enforced and
guaranteed by parties in every European Parliament
working in union with each other, insisting upon

knowing what their Foreign Offices are doing and pursuing a common policy decided upon by themselves at joint conferences held frequently. In other words, we must create a machinery of democratic diplomacy with decisions guaranteed and enforced by the mutual confidence of the peoples which only the existence of such an organization can establish. We can have Hague Courts by the score and Arbitration Treaties by the thousand, but without this diplomacy of the democracy there can be no guarantee of peace.

This organization of international democracy will seek to control the action of the various nations so that the official diplomacy, if disruptive and aggressive, will be deprived of its backing from public opinion, and will thus find its agreements and policy useless. In other words, there must be for foreign policy the same checking and controlling political organization expressing the popular will as there is for home policy, but obviously this organization must be international and not national. The general strike against war, should it ever be necessary then, will be assured by an international working-class compact so that it will not weaken one nation which resorts to it—a foolish and suicidal thing—but will prevent any military authority launching war upon the world.

Above all, this new diplomacy will trust to no armed force. It will give no support to citizen armies because it will have no need of them, or to any idea that militarism is anything but a menace to the security of a nation. It will labour under no delusion that there is a difference between military defence and offence, because it will have been taught by experience that both are aspects of the same error. People talk of an international police force as though the enforcement of law in an international State made up of a dozen or so of nations could be done in the same way as in a national State of millions of citizens. That is not so. A delinquent State, when the people have seen the futility of militarism, must in the very nature of things accept the decisions of international courts. Its people will see to that. If they do not, each State will continue to provide its own army of defence, and instead of an international police force we shall have the present condition of affairs, with all the consequences described in this book. To call national armies an International Police Force seems to me to be nothing but sticking new misleading labels upon them.

In an oration delivered in memory of Jaurès on the second anniversary of his death, M. Vandervelde spoke these words, quoting Nietzsche, " that great German who more than any one detested Prussian militarism ": " Those who fight against monsters ought to take care lest they become monsters themselves," and he added: "We fight against militarism and the spirit of conquest ; take care lest we one day become the prisoners of militarism." Europe has been the prisoner of militarism for generations, and every time it has tried to free itself it has only deepened and darkened its dungeon. Is it to repeat its past error?

NATIONAL DEFENCE

CHAPTER I

PACIFISM AND PEACE

WHEREVER the rival armies may be when this war
ends, none of the great political problems which
have produced the conflict will have been solved.
The nations will not be in a position or in a frame
of mind to dispense with armed force. They will
be exhausted; they will be horror-stricken ; they
will begin to examine the tales and the opinions
which braced them whilst the work of mutual
destruction was proceeding, and they will correct
the one and revise the other, but they will not
have rid themselves of those fears and ambitions,
those rivalries and interests, those enmities and
injuries which call for military preparations and
which ultimately use them.

This futile ending of the greatest and the most
brutal and costly war which the world has ever
known can be obviated only on one condition—
that the people of Europe settle for ever the causes
of war. If they content themselves with expressing

sentiments of peace whilst they allow policies to be pursued and obligations to be incurred which make conflict inevitable, their neglect as citizens will render their piety as individuals of no avail. Indeed, this piety will only be an added danger. For how will it work out? In the intervals between the wars the piety of pacifism will tinge public opinion, and the danger of the international policy which is again leading the nations into war will be minimized by statesmen who are at one and the same time responsible for the fateful policy and yet dependent for their authority upon electors of pacific intentions.

This heart-breaking situation when good popular intention becomes a national weakness, and when it prevents the menacing truth from being told and the proper defence from being prepared, was that in which Europe found itself in 1914 when the present war came upon it.

In Germany, where authority is stronger than in any other European State except Russia, this danger was not very great, though it was increasing. Bernhardi wrote in order to minimize it. He shared the view of the military class that a war was inevitable. He believed that Germany would have to fight to secure necessary outlets for her commerce and her people, and he believed that the encompassing Powers meant to challenge the growing influence of Germany in the world. Men brought up in a military atmosphere, whose actions and outlook are determined by military assumptions, who believe that force is the midwife of progress, would naturally take that view, and those men have more authority in Germany than elsewhere. But Bernhardi wrote because the German people threatened to become actively pacifist. They had been a military nation, he said, but " in striking contrast to this military aptitude, they have to-day become a peace-loving—an almost too peace-loving—nation. A rude shock is needed to awaken their warlike instincts and compel them to show their military strength." [1] Again : " Thus the political power of the nation, whilst fully alive beneath the surface, is fettered externally by this love of peace." And again : " From this stand-point I must first of all examine the aspirations of peace which seem to dominate our age and threaten to poison the soul of the German people." He told them of the danger they were in and, by explaining military plans and necessities, sought to enlighten them as to what he conceived to be their duty. His book fell flat, and its circulation was insignificant. But the war came before the Germans were in a frame of mind to distrust their military leaders. Their fear of Russia was known to everybody,[2] and by playing upon that the Govern-

---

[1] *Germany and the Next War*, pp. 10, etc.

[2] Bebel once told me in private conversation that if Russia attacked Germany he himself would shoulder a rifle if he could.

ment rallied the German nation into a military unit, and it fought.

But in Great Britain political sentiment was enormously stronger than military authority, and political sentiment was pacifist. It had, in consequence, to be mollified. Whilst every one who was in touch with European movements became increasingly unhappy about the outlook of affairs, the masses had to be kept quiet by pacific assurances. A handful of men trained in military thought tried to do in Great Britain what Bernhardi did in Germany, but failed. The Navy League and the National Service League saw the military implications of the international policies in which our country was mixed up, and conducted their respective propaganda. The nation refused to listen, not because it would not accept the responsibility of self-defence, but because it had to be told, and was told, by the politicians that it was not in danger. It assumed that defence meant repelling invasion, not fighting on the Continent. It was wrong—fortunately, as I shall show—but it was wrong all the same. Thus we neither got the chance of removing the danger by insisting upon a revision of international policy nor of providing for it by adequate military preparations.[1]

[1] Whoever has written or spoken with knowledge and honesty since this war has broken out has, irrespective of other opinions, agreed that the Governments have hoodwinked the nation.

The proof of this lies in the records of the
past dozen years. Nearly every increase in naval
expenditure was accompanied by the pledge that
Ministers hoped to produce reductions the next year.
Mr. Lloyd George gave the country a New Year's
message for 1914—the year when the war broke
out—in which these sentences occurred : " I think
it [this] the most favourable moment that has
presented itself during the last twenty years. . . .
Our relations with Germany are infinitely more
friendly now than they have been for years." His
misreading of the Agadir incident is plain, but
his assurances regarding it were emphatic.   It
" served the useful purpose of bringing home to
Germany and ourselves the perils involved in
the atmosphere of suspicion which had been created
and maintained by the politicians, the press, and
certain interests." Finally, he gave the country
this soothing explanation and defence of Germany's
military preparations : " The German Army is vital,

Cf. Oliver, *Ordeal by Battle*, p. 23 (abridged edition) : " The
criticism against British foreign policy for upwards of a century
is that it has aimed at managing our international relations on a
system of hoodwinking the people." That on the one side ; this,
from the *Manchester Guardian*, December 3, 1912, on the other :
" Too much blame is laid on the newspapers for the part they
play in provoking international misunderstandings, for no one
is more ready to use them for its own purposes than the Foreign
Office itself and its agents abroad, and if half-truths often do
mischief, the fault is with the methods of diplomacy for con-
cealing the rest."

not merely to the existence of the German Empire but to the very life and independence of the nation itself, surrounded as Germany is by other nations each of which possesses armies almost as powerful as her own." The only effect, and surely the only intention, of these words was to lull the nation into a comfortable restfulness.

But the most conclusively apposite proof of my contention is found in two speeches delivered by Mr. Asquith. In 1912 Lord Haldane went to Berlin to try to come to some agreement with Germany after the very serious friction over Morocco. Mr. Asquith referred to Lord Haldane's mission and the subsequent negotiations, during a debate on Imperial defence in the House of Commons [1] as follows :—

Our relations with the great German Empire are, I am glad to say, at this moment—and I feel sure are likely to remain—relations of amity and goodwill. My noble friend Lord Haldane, the present Lord Chancellor, paid a visit to Berlin early in the year. He entered upon conversations and an interchange of views there which have been continued since in a spirit of perfect frankness and friendship, both on one side and the other, and in which, I am glad to say, we now have the advantage of the participation of a very distinguished diplomatist in the person of the German Ambassador.

When the war broke out, Mr. Asquith, speaking in Cardiff,[2] referred to the Haldane conversations

[1] July 25, 1912, *Hansard*, p. 1393.
[2] October 3, 1914.

and the interchange of views which followed in a diametrically opposite sense :—

They [the German Government] wanted us to pledge ourselves absolutely to neutrality in the event of Germany being engaged in war, and this, mind you, at a time when Germany was enormously increasing both her aggressive and defensive resources, and especially upon the sea. They asked us—to put it quite plainly—they asked us for a free hand so far as we were concerned, if, and when, they selected the opportunity to overbear, to dominate, the European world.

In peace, public opinion demanded some pledge that we were at peace, and the pledge was given through the House of Commons; at war, a justification for the war had to be given, and the very same circumstances which justified a pacific statement in 1912 were made to justify a belligerent statement in 1914. This proves that whilst the nation was drifting into war the nation itself was not only asleep but was being kept asleep. During these critical years we had the most specific assurances that we were in no entanglements, that we had no commitments, that we never signed secret treaties, and none of the assurances were reliable.

The unwillingness of a people to accept militarism will not enable them to avoid it. Certain political policies must be supported by force, and if these policies are under the control of Government departments inspired by the methods, the traditions and the staffs of the Foreign Offices of

Europe—in the very nature of things the people who are to supply the force must be kept ignorant of the policy. This fact lies at the threshold of every profitable discussion of peace. The pieties of a peace movement which stops at sentiment delude the country during peace and are swept away during a war. They prevent honesty before a war and are no safeguard to reason and reflection when a war has come.

Therefore the people need knowledge, and they need power. If they do not get these, they will have to accept militarism, and they should not be under any delusion as to the kind of militarism which is to be their lot.

CHAPTER II

NATIONAL DEFENCE AND A CITIZEN ARMY

JUST before the war broke out two very important books were published in France, *L'Armée Nouvelle*, by Jaurès, and *Faites un Roi sinon Faites la Paix*, by Marcel Sembat, now a member of the French Cabinet. Jaurès' book—very lengthy and somewhat prolix—contained an extraordinarily fresh exposition of military tactics and organization based upon three propositions:—

1. that the army should be a citizen force ;
2. that its tactics should be those of defence, not offence ; and
3. that only when the army is a citizen force can the policy of the country be defensive.

The way in which many of the ideas explained in the book seemed to have anticipated what actually happened in the war drew great attention to it, and an abstract of it has been published in English for the purpose of inducing Labour in

particular to accept the National Service which
it advocates for France.[1]

Jaurès' position regarding Great Britain, however, must not be misunderstood. I have had many
conversations with him on the subject, and he
never expressed to me the view that what was
best for France was also best for England. At
International Socialist Congresses, when military
discussions were on, he always excluded England
from his proposals. *L'Armée Nouvelle* was
addressed to France and to countries with large
standing armies and continental frontiers. His
references to Great Britain in the book are of a
special kind.[2] He describes the Lord Haldane
reorganization of the Army, and considers that
unless European policy changes it is only a tran-
sition form, and that a militia system must finally
be evolved. He discusses the National Service
League's proposals of universal service and suspects
them. " If I were to speak quite candidly," he
says,[3] " I do not believe that peace is the chief
consideration of Lord Curzon and his friends."
They would not be sorry if something so upset
the minds of the British people that they would
plunge into war. He regards the whole movement here as an Imperialist and aggressive one.
" It is an effort to capture for political Imperialism

[1] Published under the title of *Democracy and Military Service*
[2] Pp. 496–515.   [3] P. 512.

the forces of democracy." [1] More specifically he points out that Great Britain has an alternative:—

In any case I repeat that England must either aid the movement to inaugurate a new policy which will result in agreements to disarm, and which will dissipate the nightmares of war and invasion, or accept universal service by the force of events, by the implacable logic of an armed peace, and by the dull fever of an Anglo-German conflict.[2]

The meaning of this is quite clear. Jaurès hoped that we would pursue a peace policy, and keep out of the politics and antagonisms which compelled the rest of Europe to resort to universal military service, whilst being perfectly convinced that if we did not do that the implacable logic of events would drive us into a militia system. The author of *L'Armée Nouvelle* did not wish us to adopt his system except as a last resort, and after we had failed to pursue the political policy, which he advocated and which he believed was open to us.

The book which his friend and colleague, Sembat, wrote was the political supplement to *L'Armée Nouvelle*. In a sentence its contention is that political policy—not war preparations—not military organization, determines peace and war ; that if nations have to trust for their defence to arms during peace they create, not only an undemocratic spirit amongst their people, but must also adopt

[1] Pp. 512-13. [2] P. 514.

a national organization other than democratic: " Make a King or make Peace." This is the evolution which is inevitable, and from that point of view he criticized adversely the Entente and the policy of France.

In these books we have two great Frenchmen, both devoted friends of peace, discussing from different angles the problems of peace. " Create a peace army," says the one, " because European policy threatens you, and you must defend yourself." " Create a peace policy," says the other, " because militarism threatens the very State which it is called in to aid."

Between these two magnets of fear and reason the peace sentiment swings. It creates an army to defend itself, and it supplements its military efforts by diplomatic alliances ; at the same time it sighs for a policy which will remove dangers and make military precautions unnecessary. Here is the fix in which nations are ; and the question which very few people consider, but which long experience thrusts upon us is, Can a nation swinging between these two policies ever have peace? Can a Jaurès ever assist to write history as both he and Sembat would like it to be written?

I think not, and I believe the reason to be as plain as any reason ever can be.

One of several unreal distinctions which Jaurès makes is that if the army is a citizen force, such a force would be more pacific and less under the control of diplomatists and aggressive military sections than a barrack army or a hired one. In other words, he argues that a citizen army is a peace army, and that statesmen can use it only for defence because it will not tolerate a war of aggression. That is not true. The argument was a familiar one at International Congresses, but this war has disproved it. No people even *make* war, whether they have to fight themselves or only pay others to fight for them. But having said that, we have said nothing of any value or importance. There was little difference in the way that the people of Great Britain, France, and Germany leaped to the sword in the autumn of 1914, and if there was any difference in the policies of the various Governments during the negotiations which preceded the war, it was the Government with the voluntary and the hired Army which hesitated most, the Government which believed that it would only have to supply a few hundred thousand men to do its share of the fighting. If there was any difference in the popular desire for peace during the last ten years, no one can say that the British people, who did not expect to have to fight as a whole, were more bellicose than either the French or the Germans. Indeed, what happened rather proves that the more general the military service is, the more readily the people accept the military assumption that war cannot be avoided, the more do they become accustomed to take it for granted that soldiers will be used to settle international quarrels. Nor is there anything in the argument that if people have to fight themselves they will be more careful to see that the sword is only the last resort. Whether they fight or only pay, their Governments have to persuade them that they have justice and righteousness on their side, and that they are defending themselves and not transgressing on other people's rights. It was a nation that Napoleon led to threaten Europe, and not a hired or a barrack army. Jaurès for a moment forgot his French history. On the other hand, when people know that they themselves have to fight, they more readily accept doctrines of " military necessity." The military argument that Belgium had to be used as a highway in order to save the lives of German soldiers was listened to more readily by Germans because the whole nation was liable to be called out than if only 4 per cent. of it had been soldiers.

Further, Jaurès simplified his categories of war when he assumed they were either offensive or defensive. They may also be casual in the sense that they have arisen out of general policy and represent a conflict in ideas or purpose. Wars in these modern days are most likely to come like the harvest of fate in a Greek tragedy. A mistake is made, an evil is done, and the innocent are dragged in to wipe out the stain with their blood. Whether the army is voluntary, and hired or citizen and conscript will make no difference in that quarrel. If there is an army there will then be a fight.

Therefore, when Jaurès says that "a nation in arms is necessarily a nation actuated by justice and uprightness," and that in consequence it will only engage in wars of defence or of liberty, he is saying what is not true, and is using high-sounding words which mislead people. Whether a nation is trained in arms or trusts in a voluntary army, its rulers are under the same necessity to gain public opinion and passion in support of war, and the former nation presents fewer difficulties to such rulers than the latter. A nation in arms thinks more in camps, and obeys involuntarily the impulses of militarism more readily than does a nation not in arms. If this argument is sound, practically the whole of the ground upon which *L'Armée Nouvelle* rests is knocked away.

This is of special importance to Labour. Under the promise that a citizen force is a peace force Labour is being invited to support national compulsion. The only result will be that the citizen Army will teach obedience and military necessity to the people, and cripple their initiative and independence, and rob their political strength of authority as it did in the case of the German Social Democrats. Universal military training does not raise any barrier of public opinion against war ; it only tends to make all public opinion pliable to authority.

CHAPTER III

NATIONAL DEFENCE AND NATIONAL OFFENCE

THE argument of the last chapter is well supported by recent events, but it requires to be elaborated. Sembat says in his book :—

I know men, reflective, cultured, perspicacious, excellent Frenchmen, who, in their secret minds or in the public expression of their thoughts, wish for war. And I know others (and those are very great in number) who, less decided and more hesitating, inclining ordinarily to peace, clench their teeth at certain times and growl, "After all, if the Germans force us——"

That is the true description of the feelings of a nation during an armed peace.[1] Some few in all nations want war; they see it is inevitable ;

[1] Another from a different quarter may be added. A writer in the *Nouvelle Revue*, one of the leading French platforms of intellectual opinion, wrote at the Morocco time :—
"We intend to have war. After forty years of heavily armed peace we can at last utter this opinion. . . . France is ready to strike and to conquer, as she was not ready forty years ago, and as she will not be in four or five years to come, owing to the annual divergent numbers of the birthrate in each country. . . . We, the attacking country, will have arranged with England that their Fleet . . . will follow the remains of the whole German Navy into German waters."

they do nothing to avert it; they let it come; they are interested only in preparing for it; when it comes they say, " Had it not been for us you would not have been so fit to fight as you are— and then where would you have been? " But the masses of all countries believe in peace and talk of peace. Jaurès upon this laid down what to me is the utterly false proposition that an army can be raised by a first-rate Power for purely defensive purposes, and that then that Power can direct its diplomacy also for purely defensive ends.[1]

I write advisedly " a first-rate Power." Such countries as Switzerland or Belgium may arm themselves for defence. They are small; they have no influence on the diplomacy which deals with the clash of great world interests. They are not, on account of their resources, Imperially minded. They have the psychology of the small State. Defence to them is something quite apart from offence, unless they are foolish enough to enter into alliances, when they may have to accept offensive

---

[1] His argument was inconsistent; for whilst he thought that England should keep out of the ring of armed nations, he argued that France could best keep the peace by being armed, and so compelling her people to interest themselves in policy. I should have thought that if his conclusions about France were sound, England, too, would have been doing the peace of Europe a service if she had armed herself in order to bring the pressure of an interested public opinion to bear upon her Foreign Office. But that is in passing.

responsibilities. Then, however, when they are attacked no defence can save them; it cannot be effective for its purpose.

But where a Great Power, like Germany, France, Russia, or ourselves, is concerned, defence and offence are so intermingled that it is a mere academic abstraction to discuss the two as though they issued in separate policies. " The best defence is often offence " is a sound military maxim; it is a law in military tactics. But it is also a law in diplomacy. It becomes a necessity imposed on both sides when the accumulated burdens and fears of efficient defence call for some action to put an end to the unbearable strain. The man in the street who accepts newspaper origins of war is therefore always misled.

A policy of defence presupposes that some one else is pursuing one of offence. There is always a potential enemy against which the threatened nation measures itself. The defending country not only arms itself but supplements its military equipment by military diplomacy. It chooses armed friends who accept the alliance for reasons of their own. National alliances are, as an almost universal rule, *mariages de convenance*.

Thus France made an Alliance with Russia the terms of which have never been published, but which the world has been given to understand was for defensive purposes. The logical result of this is the Balance of Power. In this way, nations group themselves into two camps, both of which justify, themselves on the grounds that they are defensive, and are accepted for that reason by the various peoples involved in them. But the policy of alliances is complicated. It cannot be purely defensive; its motives must be mixed. Historically, the Triple Alliance was defensive; but it developed into an offensive. Who will make bold to say, that in reality the Franco-Russian Alliance was purely defensive? Each member of the Alliance has its own aims and policies, which it advances through the Alliance.

In any case, a time comes in the evolution of events when the armed force becomes an influence on political policy. An army being in existence, policy is influenced by the possibility of its use. By and by defence requires, and becomes, hostile action. One of the parties requires to expand, perhaps; it needs a new form of armament, as the Triple Alliance needed a sea power. Or one of the parties—like Austria—becomes involved in an offensive policy. The result is that by a process of subtle development the steps taken for defence produce a condition of war between the whole of the two camps. The very thing which the arms and the alliances were designed to avoid has been brought about by them. They produce the dreaded catastrophe, and at the same time, by meeting it,

seem to justify themselves. Thus, assuming that
France had become really pacific before 1914, and
that all intention of wiping out the disgrace of the
Sedan and the loss of Alsace-Lorraine had vanished
from the nationalist French mind, the political situation that year, when the Austro-Balkan or Teuto-
Slav troubles came to a head, was such that France
could not keep out of a European war. The
defensive alliances had gathered round themselves,
and got mixed up with, causes of dispute in which
their partners took opposing sides and which, in
consequence, were extended from the Balkans into
the whole of Europe. The position then was, so
far as France was concerned, " If Russia fights,
we must fight too "; so far as Germany was concerned, " If Russia fights, France, too, will come
in, so our military plans must be laid accord-
ingly." The holding back of French troops to
within ten kilometres from the frontier at the outbreak of hostilities between Russia and Germany,
was, therefore, an act of no value whatever—an
act which could have had no effect upon subsequent military events. It did affect the political
situation, however, and brought public opinion on
to the side of the Government. " The French
Ambassador gave me to understand that France
would fulfil all the obligations entailed by her
alliance with Russia, if necessity arose, besides sup-
porting Russia strongly in any diplomatic negotia-

tions," [1] wrote Sir G. Buchanan to our Foreign Office as early as the 24th July. So with us. Sir Edward Grey said quite truly that the attitude of Germany to Belgium would not have a decisive effect upon our action, though it would influence it.[2] The determining effect was the fact that we were in the Entente and that it was a military alliance. Our honour had been privately bound to see France through in a war with Germany. But the German—still more the Austrian—State, being more militarist in its authority than that of either France or Great Britain, could begin the war by purely military moves, whilst France and Great Britain had to begin it with political moves. Germany lost the war largely because it forgot civilized public opinion; the Allies gained it because they had to pacify the opinion of their people, and, as a by-product, gained that of the world. If Germany had not been so responsive to " military necessity " she would have hesitated before she invaded Belgium and forgot humanity in her eager pursuit of military advantage. That would have made no difference so far as the number of the nations engaged in the war (except for Belgium herself) is concerned, but it would have made all the difference in the world so far as public opinion is concerned.

[1] White Paper No. 6.
[2] White Paper : Documents 119, 123.

But the real fact remains that when the Balkan squabble became a Russian quarrel, France could not then rest upon her sword; when the Balkan weakness became a Teuton irritation and temptation the Alliance, not Austria or Germany alone, acted. The Alliance and the Entente had to fight.

The error in Jaurès' argument that a citizen army can only be an army of defence is therefore shown in every sentence which describes the position of France just before this war broke out. Jaurès assumes that the will of the people makes war. The will of the people is like a leaf floating on the current; it must drift with the stream and go whither the rush drives it. When public opinion settles policy, armies are secondary affairs. When militarism settles policy, public opinion at any given moment is a secondary affair, though it must always be considered.

The same is true as regards Great Britain. Consulting Parliament on the 3rd August, 1914, was a mere formality. It was not a real consultation, because the die had been cast before it took place. The soldier was already in the saddle, but it was necessary for him to pay his respects to Parliament. Great Britain was in the Entente; she had shared in the policy of the Entente; she had to side with the Entente. An event like the invasion of Belgium had no more influence in deciding if the Entente would fight as a whole than a shower of rain had.

It affected public opinion at the moment; it did
not determine national policy. The statement made
by Lord Hugh Cecil in *The Times* on the 29th April,
1916, that the war was decided, " not by the House
of Commons or by the electorate but by the con-
currence of Ministers and ex-Ministers " is true
to the letter. We were on the brink of war over
Morocco in 1911 and 1912 just as we were in
July 1914, and in 1911-12 Belgium had never
been mentioned. In fact, whatever doubt Germany
ever had as to whether the invasion of Belgium
would bring us into the war in 1914, she never
had the least doubt in 1911 that she would then
have had to fight us. If the war had broken out
then, public opinion would have been enlisted on
some other issue. The simple truth is—and to
believe in any other theory is only to humbug
ourselves and other people—that the Alliance and
the Entente came into conflict because preparations
for war and a military policy of defence must
always issue in war and provide a reason for war.

The truth I have been setting forth, that when
war is made by policy it is impossible, while
armies exist, for the people to think and act inde-
pendently of the circumstances in which they find
themselves, is enforced very substantially by the
way in which the peoples living under a foreign
sovereignty obeyed that call in 1914. The Russian
Pole, for instance, marched with the Russian, the

Prusssian Pole with the German, the Austrian Pole
with the Austrian Army. The various races of
the Austro-Hungarian Empire filled the Austrian
Army as though they had no internal discords.
The outbreak of war draws all people round their
sovereign authority, because in the flame of its
emotions all differences are fused. Every country,
is believed to be in the right by its own people,
and the objection to being conquered is for the
time being the greatest of all objections.

Another attempt to maintain the false distinction
between defence and offence is found in the use
to which the armed citizen is put. Before the
war the National Service League insisted that it
only wished to apply conscription for home defence,
and the Territorials were enrolled for that purpose.
But what did the distinction amount to when the
war broke out? The Territorial who resisted the
pressure put upon him to offer himself unreservedly,
had either to have an overwhelming reason for
holding back, or was branded as a coward and his
life made miserable. When war breaks out an
armed and a trained man will, either by law or
social pressure, be compelled to become a soldier
who fights where his rifle is required and not where
he himself selects. A home defence force is poten-
tially an expeditionary force. Soldiers like Lord
Roberts and Lord French have always expressed
that opinion. Only the civilian was allowed to

remain under any delusion—till the war broke out.

Therefore the distinction which Jaurès made between a military policy for defence and a military policy for offence is altogether unreal and artificial. The truth is that so long as we have armies, whatever may be the justification we plead for them, we shall have wars. The kind of army will not determine how it is to be used. If we once admit that force is necessary for national defence, then every other militarist evil follows. The defence must be complete and professionally able—hence compulsion; the diplomacy which supplements it must play into its hands—hence alliances, secrecy, and Balance of Power; the political psychology which supports it must not weaken it—hence a military caste exercising independent authority in the democratic State. If defence depends on force, then it is criminal, it is treason, to feed the country on honeyed words, on dishonest ideas, on false pacifist piety. For the force must be equal to its work, otherwise it is not defence, and the enemy knows it. The State trusting to force has to turn to force and say, " What you need for your sustenance I must give you, and be content with the remnant of political liberty which is left." How much is left Germany shows. For this is the position of Germany : Believing that she could live only by force and expand only by force, she trusted to force rather than to negotiation. She became an Empire of force and accepted its conditions. Her defence became an offence. Thus the Great Powers of Europe became committed to war, and during the year or two which preceded its outbreak the most trivial incident might have precipitated it.

There is no halfway abiding-place between absolute peace and absolute militarism. If the nation will not listen to good counsel and establish the conditions of the former, it must accept the burdens and oppressions of the latter.

CHAPTER IV

NATIONAL SERVICE AND THIS WAR

IT is being frequently said that if the country had been wise enough to have taken Lord Roberts' advice and had adopted National Service before the war broke out, either there would have been no war or it would have been over by now with a complete victory for the Allies.

I do not believe that any one who has studied the details of the war or the diplomacy which pre-ceded it can hold such an opinion. All the facts show that the German military authorities did not consider that we could trouble them except upon the sea, and they held that opinion, not because our Army was small but because they did not believe in our military genius. Moreover, they apparently were not sure until the last moment that we would come in at all, and that uncertainty would not have been removed had our Army been large or small. A diplomatic and military situa-tion had been created in Europe which made war certain. We had either to turn back or go on

through war, and the arming of Great Britain in
1911 or 1912 [1] would not only not have eased
that situation but might have hastened the crisis.
Whatever view may be taken of the origins of the
war and of action that might have prevented it,
one thing is clear, and that is that more military
preparations would not have secured peace. Accu-
mulating armaments gradually drove home the con-
viction into the minds of all the peoples that they
were meant to be used, and as these accumulations
went on they pushed into the background all
agencies for and possibilities of peace. They were
challenges, not securities.

If no military preparations could have prevented
the war, might they not have changed its course,
shortened it, and made its ending more decisive
in our interests? Obviously had we put an army
of 1,000,000 into the field in August and September
1914 instead of one of 160,000, events would not
have been the same as they have been. Our
casualties would have been much heavier during
the first year, the costs would have been much
greater, our munition supply much less, our
industrial output greatly curtailed, and our
financial staying power substantially diminished.
All the earlier moves would have been intensified,

[1] If Lord Roberts had been listened to much earlier than
this the European chaos might have been greater than even it
is, and France might have been an enemy instead of an Ally.

4

but that does not mean that events would have
been better for us.

The course of the war as we have experienced
it has been that Germany played for a " knock-
out " blow and failed, that France and Russia presented a retreating front which yielded like elastic
but did not break, which steadily tightened and
finally began to advance again. Our part was to
keep the seas and to finance the two conscript
Powers whilst they were resisting the energetic blows
of the enemy. By and by we were to come in
with millions of men when the enemy's first blow
was spent, and when fresh troops were to decide
the military issues. That is a strategy balanced
in its parts and rationally complete and co-ordinated
—a strategy the success of which events are proving.
In war, when so much depends on chance and
victory anyhow is all that is wanted, it is nothing
more than a vain pastime to sit down and imagine
how much different things would have been had
this and that been done and not that and this;
and this pastime is all the more vain when experience has shown that the apparent shortcomings
complained of have contributed tremendously to the
success which has been won. For it is plain to
every one that had we had National Service before
the war our contribution to the campaigns would
not have been all that we have given plus something extra, but something quite different altogether.

I believe that a detailed examination of what has actually happened shows quite conclusively that the services which this country has rendered to the Alliance have been far more useful than if our first Expeditionary Force had consisted of a million men.

Had we exchanged industrial and financial help for military help what might have happened? The German " knock-out " blow would have been met by a " knock-out " blow. The reply would have failed, and the forcing of an early issue would have been to the advantage of the German military machine, which, owing to its interior position, would have benefited by rapid issues. So much so is that the case that it is more than likely that a more aggressive military strategy on the part of France and ourselves at the beginning of the war (Russia could not have been more aggressive) would have meant our ultimate defeat. As it turns out, the fact of the country having rejected Lord Roberts is the reason why this war cannot end in a German victory, because that rejection has meant that all the resources of the Allies have been poured into the fight in such ways and at such times as enabled each to give its maximum service to the combination.

If we were to build up theoretically a combination of Powers which ought to be unvanquishable, we should construct something like the Entente, which has a vast population, a mobilized army sufficient for defence, enormous financial and industrial reserves. But no sane man, having got such a combination, would ever think of making its war preparations military alone, or of making the contribution of each of the Allies uniform. Its strength and invincibility lie in the variety of its essential services, and to make it militarist throughout would be to weaken it. The strategy it would devise would not be that of the " knock-out " blow. It would open on the defensive and, with its mind fixed upon all the moves leading up to success, it would not trouble if part of its territory were in the occupation of the enemy. From a purely military point of view that has its advantages, as is seen to-day when we compare the state of public opinion in France and Germany, respectively. It is a great disadvantage to the German military, powers that no part of their country is in the hands of the enemy, because it leaves them weak in public opinion. Through the demoralization of its enemy this theoretical combination would march to success. Such a strategy gives the greatest security of success and entails a minimum of loss, but that is exactly the strategy which would have been impossible if those who favour National Service had had their way. Paradoxical though it may, seem, it is literally true to say that had we as a member of the Entente made more military preparations for war we should have run greater risks of defeat than we have done. It is really not paradoxical at all, because it is only an experience of the fact that the maximum efficiency of a combination, whether it be a football team or an alliance of States, depends upon differentiation and not uniformity of function.

Thus events have turned out. Chance—for it is nothing more than chance—has been favourable to us. We cannot flatter ourselves that we designed it because we foresaw it.

> All may be well, tho' if God sort it so
> 'Tis more than we deserve.

But I am pointing out in this book that when the war is over this country is likely to be driven into more militarism, and it may be asked whether that argument is not inconsistent with this chapter. It is not. The character of our present Alliance is lucky for us, but it would indeed be a foolish nation that would trust everything to chance because it was once favoured by good fortune.

If we were sure of allies who would put great armies into the field whilst we were financing them and training our own, we might maintain our present policy. But we can never be sure of such allies; we can never be sure where national interests are to lie ten years ahead. The history of Europe is a kaleidoscope of changing allies. Besides, the reason why the country was wise enough to reject Lord Roberts was that it did not believe that National Service was necessary for National Defence. Its decision had nothing to do with the strategy of the Allies. A nation's military policy will always be determined primarily by considerations of self-defence, and I am perfectly sure of this, that even were the argument in this chapter accepted by every rationally minded man in the country, if it were believed that there would be another war in ten years, the crowd mind would be so moved by fear and be so reluctant to take what it would call the " risk " of finding an Alliance so favourable as that of which we are now part, that it would call for the policy of the German State, seek to combine military with industrial functions, and prepare for a strategy of offence. The people of a State will always be moved by the desire to be self-contained in their means of defence, because an essential characteristic of the military idea is that no State can really trust another, but must always be prepared to stand alone or seek new friends.

Moreover, it is also doubtful if the other Allies would agree to our part. There are risks in it for them too, and when fear is abroad and the military mind is set to deal with it that mind will move in accordance with its own notions and will think of narrowly strict military equipment.

Thus we have the apparent paradox of, on the one hand, the certainty that National Service would not have prevented the war but would have diminished our chances of coming well out of it, and, on the other, the equal certainty that the war is creating political conditions and national frames of mind which, when peace comes, will make some form of conscription highly probable. The dilemma is the dilemma of militarism, which is created to give a sense of security and to defend, whereas its very existence keeps fear alive and adds to danger.

CHAPTER V

AN "ENFORCED" PEACE

AT this point it is necessary to discuss the move-ment which has been founded in America, and which has many advocates in this country, to enforce peace by an armed union of nations.

The proposal is that the leagued nations should agree to submit all differences to arbitration, that they should at the same time maintain effective armies, and that these armies should be available for the punishment of any nation which violates the basis of agreement.[1] That this is an advance

[1] An extract from the speech delivered at the inaugural meeting of the league by Mr. Hamilton Holt, editor of the American *Independent,* may be given as an indication of what is in the mind of the promoters of this League :—

" Now, suppose a League of Peace is established. Suppose the majority of the Great Powers—all the Great Powers if we can get them—should join such a League. The small Powers would have to come in for protection. Suppose the Great Powers, or the majority of them, had a standing army, we will say, of two million men. Suppose Russia stays outside of the League and has a standing army of a million men. The League, even if they thought that Russia was likely to attack it, could reduce its force down to a million and a quarter, or a million and a half, and still protect itself against Russia. But what will be happening in the

upon the present state of affairs and upon the
Balance of Power policy may be agreed. That
it is the best that should be aimed at now, in view
of the horror with which this war will have filled
the minds of the nations, is more doubtful. That
it will bring about its purpose is also doubtful.

The hopes based upon such a union of States
are, however, by no means unimportant or not
worth some effort to fulfil. They are that, granting that militarism will survive this war, it ought
to be controlled and curbed by co-operative legal
action, and not left to be played with or gambled
with by national egotism or self-will. A State
using military power will then be treated as a

meantime in Russia? Will not the Liberals notice that the
members of the League are enjoying greater protection for less
taxes, and are attempting all sorts of co-operative experiments,
perhaps even Free Trade, as did our States under our Constitution? They will forthwith begin to bring pressure to bear upon
the Russian Government, until finally Russia will apply for
membership in the League. Then, when Russia enters, there
can be a second *pro rata* reduction of the forces of the League
down to the size of the next great nation outside, and, when that
nation comes in, there will be another *pro rata* reduction, and so
on down and down, until finally a mere international police
maintains the peace of the earth, under a Federal form of
government, with legislative, judicial, and executive branches.
This is the theory of the League of Peace."

The words and the ideas of this pronouncement show the
unreality of the conception which the League has of the nature
of arms and of diplomacy. The story belongs to the fairy order.
It assumes a simplicity of motive and a removal of difficulties
which is not in accordance with reality.

dangerous citizen is and will be faced by organized authority. Thus, " the armed anarchy which preceded and led up to the war " will be controlled by an armed order, and the Ishmael who would strike will know that he will have to reckon with a combination of socially minded States who are ready to strike back and to strike all together.

Whatever we may hope for ultimately, after the war the arrangements between nations for securing peace must be made by Governments, and however much we may distrust them we ought to help them in making it difficult for themselves to fight each other again.

Also, it is argued, the mere coming together of States in this close way will begin the habit of rational negotiation, and of talking difficulties over in council with others, and that, as militarism is the expression of a frame of mind destroyed by that habit, this union of nations will gradually evolve into disarmed nations.

As I have said, if the peoples of the Great Powers of the world are unprepared for a further advance in common sense, this proposal may be an improvement on the existing state of affairs. But it is not without its special dangers, which will appear big or small according as our confidence in existing Governments is weak or strong. The whole anti-militarist section in Europe and America is not agreed as to how much confidence

can be placed in existing Governments. One wing
accepts them and believes that, with some changes
in political opinion, Foreign Offices as we know
them, industrial rivalries, scrambling for markets,
can be controlled ; another wing regards the
happenings of the past two years as the final
proof that existing governing interests, classes, and
points of view are incapable of maintaining peace
even when they are doing their feeble best to that
end, and this wing bases its hopes of the future
solely on the intelligence and determination of a
popular international movement which will not only
control but change the existing machinery of
Foreign Offices. If the peace of the world is
to be maintained these two wings must co-operate,
each doing its own work and contributing to the
common gain whatever practical results may be
achieved. Therefore, even if we cannot all support
this League, our critical attitude to it ought not to
amount to active hostility *unless it were to take
up the position that it is a sufficient end in itself.*

From the standpoints of this latter school of
opinion, the League to Enforce Peace contains in
itself all the evils of militarism, and this school
doubts if any effort to control these evils can in
the end succeed.

This new Union of nations, it must be assumed,
will be managed just as existing alliances are
managed, for it does not propose to make any

of the changes in international relations which I
think essential. It is a League of the old order
of national policy, not of the new. Within the
Union there will be alliances and understandings,
co-operations and rivalries. Outside it there will
be the disputes of diplomacies and capitalism, the
problems of markets, the campaigns of politicians,
the unremoved fears and suspicions of nations.
The Union itself will be controlled by the governing authorities of the nations, from whose point
of view its activities will be conducted. It might
even become a menace to liberty like a new Holy
Alliance. It will certainly have all the small
nations at its mercy, and whilst presumably it would
suppress rebellion, it would have no power to deal
with the demands of subject peoples striving for
liberty.

The handing over of the issues of peace and
war to an international committee of the governing
classes gives no security to the people that the
forces of the world will be used only in causes of
righteousness and liberty ; the creation of a great
international machine controlling the armies of the
world is no guarantee of peace ; militarism under
an international council would be deprived of none
of its national menace to democracy—the liberty
of the subject, the freedom of labour from military
interference in times of industrial dispute, and so
on ; and finally, an international agreement based

upon efficient national armies would tend to perpetuate the belief that armies are necessary for
security—the very assumption which I believe is
at the root of our international troubles.

If nations made war without any purpose except
the mere making of war, the League might prevent
war. But nations do not do this. We can prove
that war never pays, that it is brutal destruction,
that it is tremendously risky, and there will be
war all the same. The great eruption of passion
and enthusiasm which attends the outbreak of all
wars will set at defiance all leagues for peace
and all arbitration courts so long as that eruption
has the armed force at its hand through which
to express itself. A national military organization
backed up by a military diplomacy can always
create a situation which will defy the intervention
of courts of arbitration.

Moreover, the creation of such a Union presents
great difficulties. It can easily be a mere thing
of paper, like the Hague Conferences. Nations
would be at liberty at any time to leave it, and
their rulers, if backed by the Press, could satisfy
their people that national interests compelled them
to secede; majorities at any crisis might be
influenced to give wrong decisions; the practical
impossibility of saying what is the military efficiency
of a nation at any given moment would always make
the military programmes of such a League un-

certain, for the mere numbers of a standing army are only one of the elements in military efficiency. Rapidity of mobilization, the strategic value of railways, the training of nominally unarmed citizens, the character of the armaments, the amount of reserve munitions, the organization of the industries of a country are all vital considerations in war, and these no League can control. So far short of the best does this proposal fall that, in view of the reaction against war which this war will bring, every one who wishes to put an end to war for ever between civilized and law-abiding nations should strive for something more satisfactory and decisive than this.

If, however, it be argued that this Union pre-supposes that the people will take a close and intelligent interest in their international affairs, and that they will never again put themselves in the hands of military and diplomatic classes to mortgage their honour and accept responsibilities for them behind their backs, then that assumption supports much more drastic steps than the forma-tion of such a Union. If the people are so enlightened as to protect their interests within such a Union, if they are so vigilant as to prevent its being captured by the classes and interests and motives and policies which now make wars, they do not require it at all. They will end the very conditions which make such a Union an advance

upon the existing system of alliances and armaments.

There is one danger to the American democracy
in particular associated with this League. To
America it means " preparedness," which is but
a rechristening of the old European error that
peace is maintained by armaments, and that
national defence means the organization of force.
Now, the object of American preparedness is not
very clear, but two consequences are indisputable.
In existing frames of mind it will be disturbing
to Canada, which may reply, and thus the military
grip on the world will be strengthened and national
insecurity increased. It will also increase the
aggressive power of United States finance, especially on the American continent, and will lay United
States policy more open than ever to the designs
of the great financial houses. Whatever may be
said in Europe in favour of such a League,
nothing can be said in its favour in America, unless
it is argued that in order to help to emancipate
the Old World from militarism, the New World
should put its neck under the military yoke.

My contention is that so long as the people are
kept apart as they now are, so long as the kind of
national policies which are now pursued continue,
so long will the causes of war operate, and no
mechanical contrivance of a Union of Nations or
of legal arbitration can protect civilization against

war ; and further, that so long as these things last, any machinery controlling military power can be captured by the war - making interests and instincts. It is impossible to conceive of peace secured by courts of arbitration or by any other means so long as efficiently trained troops and an army organization are at the disposal of Governments. The currents of tendency making for war will run in new directions perhaps for a little while to come, but they will run all the same. We must not let our anchors drag if we can help it. The ground we hold is that the problem of defence is not how to protect ourselves by force against enmity, but how to remove enmity.

CHAPTER VI

NATIONAL DEFENCE AND CONSCRIPTION

THIS war will leave Great Britain with new frontiers. We thought that we started it as an island; we shall certainly issue from it as a continental Power. The Channel and North Sea are no longer our borders. It is not rhetoric but sober common sense to say that our soldiers have been fighting on the British frontiers in France and Flanders. The frontiers of nations in alliance are not those of the separate nations, but those of the alliance. The security of each is the security of the whole. The military frontier of a nation is very often outside itself.

When the war is over every effort will be made to maintain an Alliance, for we have deliberately ended the chapter of independent action and of a distinctly national world policy. The syndicate has come into politics as well as into industry. An economic war will follow, not merely to punish Germany but to keep the Alliance with France and Russia. Whether an economic alliance is good political business or not I do not discuss here. I

5

believe it is very bad political and military business. Its difficulties have been shown in our own Empire, and they will not be minimized when foreign States come in. The economic market and the channels of economic exchange cannot be coerced to suit the conveniences of military plans or of political unions, except at heavy cost and with much irritation. Neither the dangers nor the practical problems of an economic war after the war have been worked out. We are acting on a mere aggressive emotion.

What I am concerned with is to point out that after the war the military meaning of national security will not be what it was before the war, when it was the prevention of invasion. It will be that with the maintenance of the existing Alliance in addition, with its—to us—extended frontiers and increased responsibilities. Our military necessities have thus increased a great deal. I well remember that in course of conversation with an important personage some years before the war he remarked that the military road from Berlin to St. Petersburg lay through Belgium and Paris. That road has now been extended to London. To-day we seem to be assuming that when the war is over we can return to our insularity, and that, having put forth our great military effort, we can go back to 1914, so far as our military position is concerned. That is a mistake. We have changed all that. What we have had to defend during the war we shall have to prepare to defend during peace, because what was in jeopardy these two years will be in jeopardy again. National security maintained by force does not mean fighting only, but also training to fight.

Hence it is that the military problem which we once had to face, and which led to the Haldane reorganization of the Army, is now completely changed. This war has proved that in a European conflict in which we are concerned our responsibilities cannot be limited to an overwhelming naval strength, a small Expeditionary Force, and a Home Defence army of volunteers. National defence now means to Great Britain a military as well as a naval power to strike. An Expeditionary Force of 160,000 men is as much a matter of ancient history as a force armed with bows and arrows transported in fishing-boats. Jaurès' forecast regarding the evolution of the Haldane reorganization has been fulfilled.

Moreover, one new element has been added to the fighting fields—the air—and another has been transformed—the sea—by the submarine. Both of these revolutionize the military strategy for the defence of Great Britain. Our system was scrapped within the first months of the fighting. We went through months of futilities—imposed upon us perhaps by political expediency—when we appealed for recruits by posters of doubtful taste and dignity and recruiting speeches of more than doubtful intelligence and accuracy. Finally we came to the inevitable rock face of conscription. We trembled and shilly-shallied. Our rulers gave pledges that it was to be " thus far and no farther." The pledges were broken. It was " all the way." Canute went down to Southampton to prove the folly of his flattering councillors who told him that the advancing tide would obey him. To-day Canute assures his subjects that he is master over the waters. The Canute of to-day will meet with the same experience as the councillors of yesterday.

One pledge still remains unbroken—because nothing has yet clashed with it. Conscription is only for the war, we were told. That pledge, however, is likely to go with the others. It was given without thought of the new position in which the war will leave the country; it was given on the assumption that England after the war will bear the same relationship to the Continent which the people supposed it bore before the war. That is not to be so. Great Britain will remain in a continental alliance. The existing one may not last; indeed, it is not likely to last. The war will be followed by an active diplomacy inspired by the following amongst other motives. The Central European Powers will strive to form a new combination, for even a democratic Germany is likely to have memories as bitter as a democratic France had after the Franco-German War. The aristocratic and autocratic classes of the various nationalities will not continue to support an Alliance which will tend to increase the power of democracy in Europe, and the attempt to carry out the policy of the Paris Economic Conference will strengthen their hands. The new map of Europe, with perhaps Russia in possession of the Dardanelles and Constantinople, will reopen the problems of a Balance of Power and re-form the distribution of national fear and jealousy. The present Allies will, when peace comes, scrutinize the position in which the war has left them, and some little discord is certain to arise. Coalition wars have had unsatisfactory peace endings ; there are always too many interests to placate and too many weak points to defend against the diplomatic cunning of enemies.

In this new diplomacy Great Britain will appear as a military Power, and British interests will have to be defended by a British Army. We shall never again contemplate a war without an Army of decisive strength, trained, equipped, and officered. Every motive which was used on recruiting platforms, every phrase of the appeals that the nation should be defended, will continue to operate in the defensive preparations of the peace, and the universal military service of war-time will have to be continued when the war is over. There may be a year or two of a lull of exhaustion when the people are confident in the effect of their victories, but the old order will reassert itself, the old politics will produce their fears and rivalries, and the State, trusting to its military strength, will have to demand of its manhood that they become trained in the art of war.

The annual meeting of the National Service League was held on the 17th August, 1916, when Lord Milner spoke thus from the chair :—

It was impossible to carry on a propaganda in favour of a system which had already been adopted. On the other hand, it was impossible to think of dissolving so long as the question was open whether the principles for which they stood and for which a temporary triumph had been achieved were to be permanently accepted or to be thrown over again after the end of the war. They were bound to keep as quiet as they could at the present time, but they were equally bound to "keep their powder dry" in case it might hereafter be required.

Personally he had a hope that it might never be necessary for them to become again active propagandists of National Service, because the wonderful success which had attended the adoption of their principles was calculated to commend them to the nation in such a way that they would never be abandoned. That was his personal hope and belief, but, of course, they could not count on that, and must be ready and, as a body, keep together.

The old kind of opposition may be put up to this propaganda by men who accept the Paris Conference decisions, and who have not a word of criticism to offer against the foreign policy of the country before the war and who will return to a belief in voluntaryism in raising armies of defence. It will be ineffective. For unless this country emerges from the war with a new foreign policy of peace and a new conception of national defence the experience of war will drive the nation into compulsory military service, for the needs which drove us to adopt it temporarily this year will continue through the peace.

CHAPTER VII

THE MILITARY NATION

LET us disentangle our minds for a moment from the events that are now crowding thick upon us and take a wider survey.

After the French Revolution war entered upon a new phase of its development which is only still in process of evolution. By the end of the eighteenth century war had become an affair of armies, not of peoples, and, as has been said, a battle or a siege was just a form of a diplomatic note delivered by one ruler to another. When the French Republic was challenged by the rulers of Europe, they marched against it with their old armies. But the challenge was to the French people, and the French people armed themselves to resist it. Thus the modern national war began. The French armed nation was successful in defending itself, and then proceeded, with Napoleon at its head, to threaten the peoples of Europe. The peoples that were threatened responded as the French themselves had done, and Prussia, " without either money or credit, and with a population reduced by one-half, took the field with an Army twice as strong as in 1806." This revolutionized modern war. It brought in the people as well as the rulers. It established the practice of conscription. It made available for military operations the unlimited resources of the State in men and credit and labour. It can end only with the most absolute control of men, women, and children, of workshops as well as of armies, of workpeople as well as of soldiers. " Thus, therefore," says Clausewitz, " the element of war, freed from all conventional restrictions, broke loose with all its natural force." It made a public opinion in war necessary. It raised fury in the public mind. It gave a new function to the Press. It made necessary the suppression of liberty to think and speak and criticize. To the mind of nations thus placed it made the imminence of war a constant assumption. As in the Dreyfus time, an insult to the Army became an insult to the nation; as in modern Prussia, a military officer was a sacred thing apart; as in Great Britain during this war, a whisper of reason became treason to the national will.

And it must be remembered that the sources from which all this sprang was " the necessity " which the Allies a hundred years ago imposed on France, and France imposed on Prussia, to defend themselves. The origin of the European militarism of to-day is national defence, not national aggression.

The uninterrupted growth of military power in Europe throughout the century is the inevitable evolution of a false policy.

The failure of Napoleon to land in England, and the isolated position of the country ever since, protected us until two years ago from this flood of change. Part of it washed over us during the South African War; it came in its fullness during this war. No sane man can believe that it will depart when this war is over. The country mixed up in twentieth-century military diplomacy and obligations cannot possibly return to an eighteenth-century Army or an eighteenth-century attitude to war.

We can now make peace permanent or prepare for war. There is no alternative obligation. If we prepare for war, it must be for a national war involving two things—a National Army and the cultivation and moulding of opinion by the military State. For no military State can allow the growth of opinion which cuts at its own foundations. Military patriotism will be taught in schools. Patronage on the one hand and coercion on the other will be applied to our Press to keep up such education amongst the masses. The military strain and burden upon Europe will now be enormously greater than it was between 1871 and 1914. For Germany did not reach the limits of military preparation, far as she went. On its purely military

side the war has shown the need of being prepared on the vastest and the minutest scale; on
its political side it has proved the "military necessity" of creating an obedient and a muzzled people.

All the scientific modern military writers lay the
greatest stress upon public opinion, and their
thoughts are always stretching out to the final
conclusion that democracy is treason to the State,
that freedom to criticize and weaken the military
machine and its necessities is treason to the nation.
This war, described so grandiloquently as "a fight
for the right and freedom," has conquered enormous territories of the mind and of States to
militarism. We are witnessing a further stage in
the evolution of nineteenth-century militarism, not
an emancipation of twentieth-century liberty.

How the military mind is running is revealed
in an interesting interview which the Russian
General Skugarevski gave to the *Russkoe Slovo*,
and which was reproduced in the Russian Supplement of *The Times* for the 29th July, 1916, under
the heading "The Future War." "At the present
time," he says, "it is possible fairly accurately to
imagine the picture of the next war after this."
It is to be more frightful than this, both as to
scale and destructiveness. This war has brought
into the field numbers of men and masses of
munitions for which no State had made preparations. We shall begin our armament preparations

on the scale upon which this war ends them. " Humanity must at last learn how to prepare for war." This war has shown that a State will use 25 per cent. of its men for military operations. Allowing for sickness and other inefficiencies, that means that armies equal to 20 per cent. of the population will at once take the field. In ten years, therefore, the Russian Army will number 40,000,000, the German one about 20,000,000. The Russians will require 300,000 officers, who will have to be provided by a special form of conscription. It may be necessary to introduce industrial conscription for girls and childless widows, so that the places of workmen may be taken at once by women previously trained, and a supply of clothing, food, and munitions to the Army secured. The Army will be equipped with 100,000 guns, 1,000,000 Maxims, tens of thousands of motor-cars; 50,000,000 gun projectiles will have to be kept ready and 5,000,000 rifle cartridges. Each regiment will, in addition, have to be equipped with great numbers of portable machine-guns. The explosives used will be deadly in the extreme, and a tremendous advance will be made in the mechanism of rifles. There will be thousands of dirigibles and tens, if not hundreds, of thousands of aeroplanes. The daily cost of the new war on the Russian scale will be at least £20,000,000. The peace footing of the Russian Army will be

2,000,000 to 3,000,000 men, and the annual cost
will be about £100,000,000. Everything will have
to be planned during the intervening peace, and, in
preparation for the war, the labour and the industry
of the nation will have to be controlled and
organized.

We need not pin ourselves to details. The
general accuracy of this forecast is good enough.
In its evolution militarism is grasping the whole life
of the nation; everything has to be subordinate to
it; within the net it is casting, every activity and
service must be caught because all are necessary.
Those who are trusting that the pains and losses
inflicted by this war will end war are building their
houses upon sand. The memory of pain and loss
passes, and a new generation arises which has not
the memory at all. But the menace and the spirit
of militarism and of armed force endures. The
permanent memory of these years will be the need
of the most thorough preparation. This war drove
us pell-mell out of voluntaryism into compulsion,
both military and industrial, and we shall begin in
peace, not where we were in August 1914 but at
the point to which the war brought us.[1]

[1] After I had finished this book I read Naumann's *Central
Europe*, a book which in every page, argument, and proposal
shows the soundness of my position. Here there is no thought
of a settled peace. The war has made the nations more aggressive and more self-willed. " It is not to be supposed that at the
conclusion of the war the long jubilee years of an everlasting

Whether this is to happen or not, says General Skugarevski, depends upon the peace. With that we shall all agree, but we shall disagree as to what kind of peace will avoid this horror and what kind of one will make it our inevitable doom. The important thing for the moment to remember is that every responsible Government is assuming that a state of incipient war will follow the ending of present hostilities, and this will undoubtedly happen unless the people determine otherwise.

peace will begin ! . . . The war will leave behind it an immense number of unsolved problems, both new and old, and will lead to disillusionments which will express themselves in extensive armaments. All the War Ministers, General Staffs and Admiralties will ponder over the lessons of the past war, technical skill will contrive yet newer weapons, frontier fortifications will be made still wider and, above all, longer. Is it really credible that in such an atmosphere the isolated State can remain any longer in isolation?" (p. 7). Of the economic war after the war he says: "It is no theoretical academic demand but is a practical precept, and its chief supporters must be the Ministers of War on both sides" (p. 174). Further: "It will not only be Central Europe that will emerge from the war with schemes for equipment and defence, but all the other States as well. Even a growing inclination among the people towards peace can do little to alter this steady preparation for coming wars" (p. 179).

CHAPTER VIII

A DEMOCRATIC GERMANY AND PEACE

THE hope is that Germany may become democratic —perhaps a republic—as the result of the war, but I see no signs of the political genius which is handling the position with that tact which might induce the Germans to translate military defeat into a pacific democracy. We can help the Germans to do that, and we are doing the very opposite. We seem to forget that the German people may rid themselves of the Hohenzollerns and the Junkers, as the French rid themselves of their Emperor in 1871, without wishing to forget the war. The passionate hate with which it is being conducted, the flinging about of insults, the insistence that every crime committed by an army is a badge of the spirit of the whole nation, is but sowing the wind from which the whirlwind is reaped. And both sides are busy with this evil work.

The problem which Germany presents to us is as follows : We have either to exterminate it altogether or make peace with it. If we do neither the one nor the other we retain the antagonism of a people

of great energy, great mental power, great industrial enterprise, great organizing capacity, great
patience, a people, moreover, prolific in numbers.
Hampering them either by political policy or
economic manipulation is petty and futile : it only
keeps their enmity virulent. If our aim is to crush
and keep down, that spells extermination, for there
is no halfway resting-place. We cannot face, either
alone or in alliance, a generation of studied repression. Every economic war that has been fought
between States only shows the futility of those who
enter upon it.[1] A perpetual blockade is impossible,
and no political or economic means have yet been
devised for keeping an industrial country out of the
important markets of the world. A country which
has something to sell will find some one to buy.

On the other hand, we may make Germany a
co-operator in the keeping of European peace. We
may relieve Europe of the menace of German militarism and organized force, of that aggressive and
self-conscious German nationalism which threatened
to domineer over the other nations ; and at the same
time we may help to bring a feeling of freedom and
relief to the masses of Germans themselves. We
can do something of the same kind for ourselves
as well. But the methods we are adopting to keep
our people in a fighting spirit—the enflaming of
passion and the maintenance of a squabbling and

[1] See *Modern Tariff History*, by Percy Ashley.

stupid hate—threaten to defeat this. We are acting as though we deliberately wished to compel Germany to throw back in our teeth any benefits of a political kind which the war may offer to her. We are making the German people a disturbing factor in Europe, irrespective of whether democracy or militarism, the citizen or the soldier, rules in Germany. And, as I have said, the fault is not all on our side.

This is no question of saving the face of Germany, but of studying a problem and devising a solution for it. We can fight this war to an absolute military conclusion irrespective of consequences, one of the most important of which will be its effect upon the future peace of Europe ; or we can fight it with our eye fixed steadily upon its political results. We cannot do both, and nothing will be more disastrous, or will be condemned more emphatically by its consequences, than a policy (or, to write more accurately, a want of policy) which expects political results from military operations that have hitherto always brought the opposite of these results.

This war has shown that if nationalism is roused every other political impulse is swept out of people's minds. In peace times we heard much of class wars, of the capitalist being the only enemy, of patriotism being a delusion of a past age. When the war came the men who had been the most unbalanced and loud-mouthed in preaching these doctrines were blown farthest to the other extreme. Those to whom I used to protest that they were going too far, and only raising unnecessary prejudices amongst thinking people owing to gratuitous and somewhat ignorant attacks on patriotism, clothed themselves in their national flags and outdid the most Jingo of their old opponents. The Hervés of all nations are a warning that ought not to be forgotten. The German democracy is German, jealous of its national name, and will be prevented from purging itself from the blood of this war only by the attacks of foreigners.

The mere establishment of democracy in Germany will not therefore save us from having to reap the whirlwind if we now sow the wind.

The greatest weakness of democracy is that it will not think and act for itself. A race that has been conquered and kept subordinate develops the vices and virtues of subordination, and the masses and their leaders cannot in a day free themselves from the mental inheritance of subordination which their ancestors who hewed wood and drew water handed to them. When this war broke out, it was seen at once how sound were the instincts of the people and how ill-equipped were their minds. Every nation was led by its rulers, every people took up the rôle assigned to it in the military scheme. During the war the Press, whose chief work was to keep the fires of passion well stoked and blazing, published absurdities, contradicted itself, palmed off the most palpable nonsense upon the people, but the people's critical intelligence had gone to sleep. Deception was never detected because there was no memory. Thus every nation sincerely believed that it was defending itself, and that the enemy had been planning and preparing for Armageddon for years ; during the war, every people believed in the cruelties of the other ; newspaper readers knew that the censor was at work, but never paused to think what that meant as regards the news they were permitted to read every day. They must have seen that their papers were carefully selecting from enemy countries news and opinions to create prejudice, and not to reveal the real state of the enemy's mind ; and yet there was no caution shown. The people believed and did not think.

We have, therefore, to face the future and form our opinions as to what is to happen with this fact firmly set in our minds, that in matters of national security—our own old " We-want-eight-and-we-won't-wait " agitation, for instance—people are not swayed by calm judgment, but by stormy emotion and by panic. Even under a republican Germany with a grievance and a tender memory, a German Delcassé backed by the popular German Press would be an instrument for breaking the peace of Europe. And he would do this not as an avowed aggressor. There will be plenty of " causes " left unsettled in Europe after this war to give alliances an excuse for fighting—nay, even to drift alliances into war though they do not exactly wish it. I see no prospect of a final solution of Balkan difficulties ; I see no chance of a satisfactory settlement of Poland ; I see a grave menace in some of the proposed partitions of the Near East and Asia. Above all, I see no prospect of the racial enmity between Slav and Teuton being ended, no hope of removing from Europe by any of the policies now in vogue the dangers of the Pan-Slav and the Pan-Teuton conflict. A democratic Germany will, indeed, have no difficulty in finding many opportunities in the next generation to challenge the decision of this war and to write a sequel to it more congenial to the German spirit than the record that is now being made.

Happy, but profoundly mistaken, is the man who, taking up his newspaper every morning, reads of allied victories and sees in them the security of an abiding peace ; reads of German cruelties and believes that by crushing the nation and punishing the innocent and the guilty together, the responsible and the irresponsible in one sentence, he is to cut from our civilization the cancer which corrupts it. He neither diagnoses the disease nor understands the remedy. He is a quack and the victim of quacks. His emotion is good, but his common sense and judgment are far to seek. He is not only not ending Prussian or any other form of militarism :

he is handing himself over to the interests and the
logic of events which make a continuation of militarism inevitable, and which will drag this country
into the vortex. All that we see going on round
us to-day, the opinions that are being expressed
and the temper in which they are expressed, the
policies that are being pursued and prepared for
the coming of peace, make militarism an essential
condition of national security, and continental
alliances and counter-alliances necessary consequences.

It is true that our people have no intention of
making this war the parent of militarism, and the
words they use and the feelings which possess them
are moral and pacific. The sermons they preach
to themselves are as usual right, but there is a conduct as well as a sentiment of piety, and that is
generally forgotten. Our good intentions sometimes
become the very reason why we allow evil to be
done.

One of the reasons for this is that when a nation
is under the control of emotional piety it is apt to
forget that it was ever under such a control before.
But during wars it is always under such control.
The Allies in the Napoleonic wars proclaimed their
purpose to be " the reconstruction of the moral
order," " the regeneration of the political system
of Europe," the establishment of " an enduring peace
founded on a just redistribution of political forces."

Nationality was to be preserved and respected, treaties were to be sacred documents, war was to be ended by arbitration and a Concert of Nations. The war was fought, the peoples suffered for their ideals, Napoleon was crushed, and none of the moral intentions were fulfilled. Revolutionary and Liberal ideas were repressed, and a book which by numerous examples of *suggestio falsi* offers wrong explanations for this war [1] has to admit that when this great moral effort was ended " the rewards of that overthrow [Napoleon's], however, were reaped, not by the peoples but by the dynasties and State systems of the old *régime.*"

The moral appeals to the nation to support the Crimean War were equally conspicuous. *The Times* of the 30th March, 1854, declared that we were fighting because " of the sympathy of this people with right against wrong " and to save Europe " from the predominance of a Power which has violated the faith of treaties and defies the opinion of the civilized world." The day before it had spoken of Russia as " menacing nothing less than the conquest of all Europe." Mr. Sidney Herbert said in the House of Commons (25th July, 1854) that we were fighting for " guarantees which might afford a prospect of peace for the future." The *Illustrated London News*, attacking America for not having come in on the side of the Allies, told that country,

[1] *The War and Democracy*, p. 31.

in words which those used to-day do but echo, that it ought to have been "unanimous in support of Great Britain and France in their disinterested and generous struggle against the wicked aggressor [Russia] and disturber of the world's repose." What harvest was reaped from these words and emotions? What guarantee of peace did the Crimean War give? Historians are unanimous about that. Their verdict is expressed by Sir Spencer Walpole :—

From 1856 to 1878 the continent of Europe was afflicted with five great wars—the Franco-Austrian of 1859 ; the Danish of 1864, the Austro-Prussian of 1866, the Franco-German of 1870, and the Russo-Turkish of 1878—all of which can be lineally traced to the war of 1854.[1]

Lord Salisbury supported the historians when he said that in the Crimean War we had backed the wrong horse.

Wars can never be fought unless the peoples involved believe they are fighting for liberties or for some generous moral issue, but these great purposes have never been secured as the result of wars. There is nothing new in our spirit and our manifestos to-day. They have been published again and again. There will apparently be nothing new in the results. Nor is there anything new in our expectation that after the war our enlightened enemies will come to us in white robes of repentance, confessing that they were wrong all the time and we

[1] *Cambridge Modern History*, vol. xi. p. 324.

were right. There will be nothing new about the
way in which that expectation will be falsified, and
yet we base all our hopes of the German future upon
some such confession after a good defeat !

Germany may become a republic next year. The
Kaiser may be sent to St. Helena, the military castes
to till fields and reap harvests. But unless statesmanship settles the peace there will be no peace,
and unless public opinion accepts the terms with no
hot feelings in its heart, a German democracy will
polish and sharpen the sword and manipulate
diplomacy as effectively as any other form of government. The Jingo may rage tumultuously and the
people imagine a vain thing, but their ends will
elude them. They will never gain what they desire.
" Striking at one another desperately," said Jaurès
in 1905 of Germany and Great Britain, " the two
peoples would bruise and wound one another and
splash the world with blood ; but neither of them
would eliminate the other, and after an exhausting
struggle they would still have to reckon with one
another." This great problem of national conflict
is not to be settled by those who stumbled into it in
August 1914 for the first time and have acquired
all the information they know about it by reading
war news since then.

CHAPTER IX

MILITARISM AND DEMOCRACY

AGAIN let us widen our view from closely pressing
events. War and militarism are not the result
of the actions of rulers of evil intent. It is necessary so to stage the tragedy to-day before the
crowds, so that the theatre—stalls and galleries
together—may hiss the villains, call for the hang-
man in the final act, and be treated to a tableau
with a gibbet in the centre and a crowd of the
angelic virtues—the audience themselves—surrounding it to see that vengeance is done, and so be
assured that God is in His heaven. That is war
seen through the bloodshot eyes of war. That is
romance. That is not how military statesmen look
at it. That is neither the place nor the emotion
they assign to it. To all the greater writers and
thinkers on war, war is a mere inevitable incident
in political policy, for which much has to be said
by way of praise. It is by no means generally
regarded as an evil. It is accepted as a good.
Its training is advantageous. It licks the loafer
into shape, it braces up the slacker, it makes

men obedient and fits them for working smoothly in a machine. In other words, it substitutes mechanical discipline for self-discipline, it gives us obedience for initiative. To democracy that is an evil ; to autocracy it is a gain, because it removes the problem of training from education and assigns it to drill. But those who find good in war as a rule contemn democracy, and what they approve we naturally disapprove.[1]

Others, again, are quite open in their advocacy of militarism, on the ground that it will keep the working classes in their place and subordinate them to " higher ". interests and commands. An utterance which gained some notoriety at the time was that of Colonel Sir Augustus FitzGeorge, son of the late Duke of Cambridge, when he said at the United Service Club on the 26th August, 1915, " Compulsory service is necessary at this

---

[1] I do not accept the argument that training in the Army is good. The open air is of course all to the good, and so are the walking and the exercise. But M. Daumont, the Editor of the *Libre Parole*, has written of France that its military system " has gone a long way towards ruining our peasantry, and to a large extent has already debased them. I deem the universal military service, as it is sometimes termed, one of the saddest sacrifices our country calls on us to bear." Lieutenant Bilse's descriptions of the effect of militarism on young German soldiers in his *Life in a Garrison Town* are also well known. The men of our Empire, outwardly improved in physique by the training they have had in camp, have other sides to present to us which we shall be in a better position to examine and discuss when peace comes.

time when the people are getting out of hand."
But leaving such expressions of casual offensive-
ness out of account, there can be no doubt but
that such opinions as that expressed by Lieutenant-
Colonel W. H. Maxwell in the *Outlook* [1] are not
only prevalent but represent a large body of intelligent and weighty opinion—even if we should
call it prejudiced:—

> The abuse of personal freedom has reached its climax in this
> country. Trade Unionism—that shelter for slinking shirkers—
> is imperilling our existence, and by its action a rot of our national
> soul has set in. One remedy and one alone can eradicate this
> state of rot—martial law will cure it.

In a more general way Colonel Ross has expressed the military view. The great weakness
of the British Army, he indicates with much truth,
is that British militarism has always been subordinate to British liberty. The officer here is of no
special account as in Germany—except for dances.
And, therefore, if we are to be strong and well
protected, our military must be granted increased
respect in the country and authority in the State ;
it must have at its head a military man and not
a civilian ; representative government must not
interfere with its mind or its preparations ; military
efficiency needs the establishment of autocratic
government " in all primary questions, or those

[1] Quoted by Mr. Bruce Glasier in *Conscription*, p. 15 (Independent Labour Party, 1d.).

relating to war or the struggle for existence, and
representative government in all secondary matters
on which the comfort of the people depends." [1]   So
it must settle the framework of our Constitution.
On similar lines we have opinions like that expressed by Professor Ridgway of Cambridge in
his Presidential Address to the Classical Associa-
tion in 1915, that a world of democratic States
would be " a stagnant pool " in which no higher
forms of life could live, and that humanity in a
world of peace " would perish from its own physical
and moral corruption."

This professorial utterance puts in an academic
form an opinion and determination which were
not at all uncommon before the war, and which
were frightened by the menacing success of the
Labour Party. The only way to prevent the capture
of the State by the people was to make war.
The French agents in Germany reported to Paris,
according to the French official paper on the war,
that the Prussian Junkers welcomed war because
they were getting afraid of death duties, democracy,
and Socialism.[2]   In war the masses " substitute
national passions for social aspirations," because
war rouses the most instinctive fears of men.
Whatever the immediate cause of a war may be,
when it comes it compels some enemy to threaten

[1] *Representative Government and War*, p. 107.
[2] French Yellow Book, Document No. 5.

national existence and honour, and then the complete fabric of democratic gains and aspirations, built upon the foundations of national security, tumbles down to the ground. When the war is over, reaction has a breathing space, for the world in which democracy begins afresh to rebuild its habitations is a new and a strange one. Democratic experience has been buried deep under military emotions. Old opinions have to be revised, old principles have to be applied in new ways, democracy itself has been broken. So time is lost and the work of a generation wiped out. Reaction remains in possession until new democratic movements have been formed, programmes and policies revised, and leaders found. Thus the world drags on its weary way, the motto of reaction each generation being: " Sufficient unto the day is the opportunity thereof." A people requires to be revolutionary to the core to resist the strength which a war gives to reaction. Franchise reform very often follows wars. But then it is safe, because the democracy is in no mind to use its new powers, and being disorganized and having no certain and fixed aim, it cannot employ them to its own advantage.

We have been hitherto inclined to minimize the influence of such military and reactionary opinions as the above, just as we minimized the dangers of a war. But they have been very widespread and have been found in high and influential places. Intellectually as well as practically militarism is antagonistic to the liberty for which democracy stands ; it has to limit that liberty in its own self-interest, and it is used by other interests to the same purpose.[1]

The opinion of the soldier one understands and respects. The soldier desires the efficiency of his profession. Popular assumptions that national defence rests ultimately on force compel the soldier to study the organization of force, and he is driven to the Prussian conclusion. He naturally detests politics and politicians because their methods and psychology are poles asunder from his. He sees that the officer must be put on a pedestal, that military uniform should be a sacred garb. He wants no humanitarian humbug. The Clausewitz formula, " War is an act of violence which in its application knows no bounds,'' is honest. It has been formally accepted by the soldier of every nationality. His work is to kill, frighten, and destroy. His authority is not that of the State or the nation, but the War Council, which he demands should be composed of military men. International

---

[1] The story of the persecution of Mr. Bertrand Russell can be placed alongside the most obnoxious suppressions of civil liberty in Germany, and not suffer by the comparison. There will be a chapter in the history of this war on civil liberty, and it will read just as the similar chapter in the history of the Napoleonic wars reads.

law is a mere fiction "hardly worth mentioning."
Treaties are only valid so long as convenient.[1]
Might is to him right—at any rate, they are so
mixed up that they cannot be distinguished. In
the military mind, as Colonel Ross has said:
" Might has taken the place of right, and should
the destruction of homes and farms not prove
sufficient, whole towns must be destroyed and the
inhabitants must hang " ; or as Lord Wolseley,
dealing with another aspect of military moral
psychology, has written in his *Soldier's Pocket-
book*, that though public opinion condemns false-
hood, detests the word " spy " and believes in
honesty, " the man who acts upon that opinion
in war had better sheathe his sword for ever."
Similar expressions could be quoted through pages
upon pages. They all prove that the professional
military psychology in every country is precisely
the same. There is no distinction in spirit between
Prussian militarism and any other militarism.
Openly by practice in Prussia, theoretically in
Great Britain up to now, but now rapidly becoming
practical, militarism challenges democracy, de-

---

[1] "Directly circumstances change—and they change constantly—the most solemn treaties are torn up, as Russia tore up
the Treaty of Paris, or as Austria tore up the Treaty of Berlin.
All history is full of torn-up treaties. And as it has been, so it
will be. The European waste-paper basket is the place where
all treaties eventually find their way" (Major Stewart Murray,
The Reality of War, p. 110).

mands an independent existence in the democratic
State, and claims a morality and a rationality all
of its own. Jaurès never wrote a truer sentence
than this—true not merely as a description of what
had happened, but true as a warning of what
must always happen in the nature of things: " Who
is most menaced to-day by the military action of
the generals, by the always glorified action of
military repression? Who? The People."

Nor must we treat too lightly or too senti-
mentally the rationality of all this. These people
believe that wars cannot be avoided. Wars are
not brought about by Kaisers, but by nature. War,
says Major Stewart Murray in his interesting and
(granting his assumptions) profoundly true com-
mentary on Clausewitz,[1] " is based on the essential
fundamental characteristics of human nature, which
do not alter." We can arbitrate on non-essentials,
but we cannot arbitrate on honour. Here is the
dilemma. Honour compels us to make war ;
we make it successfully, and our military victory
forces the other side, which of course cannot accept a defeat on a point of honour, to
devise how to make another appeal to the sword.
That is the *reductio ad absurdum* of war as an
incident, as well as a determining factor, in national
policy. That *reductio ad absurdum* is, however,
accepted by the militarists as " the inherent weak-

[1] *The Reality of War,* p. 68.

ness of human nature " ; but a weakness which
is seen, exposed, and can be provided against
is not " inherent."[1]

Let us honestly face the logic of facts, however. We base national security upon an army,
and national security is psychologically an over-
mastering demand of civic human nature. So long
as the fear of national insecurity is in people's
minds, liberty and everything else must be limited
by military efficiency, the soldier acquires a privi-
leged place in the State, and the moral and intellectual requirements of his profession are accepted
as a necessity. Thus arises the doctrine of
" military necessity," which means that the military
mind is allowed to create standards of moral action
and political policy which accord with its own
problem of how to make Might and Force
triumphant. The evolution in the military
ascendancy in States, extraordinary as its results
are, is to be explained by the simplest and most
obvious psychological processes. " I am an absolute necessity," argues the soldier, " and you must
therefore allow me to create the political conditions
under which I can do my work efficiently. If
you do not do that, your blood be upon your own
heads."[1]

We can go on encouraging this idea by harbour-
ing false views of international relations, by trusting
our security to organized force instead of to

organized rationality, and by obscuring the facts and applying adjectives like " Prussian " to a spirit which is universal ; but the penalty we shall have to pay is that which is now being meted out to Germany.

How literally true it is that the people who trust to force will perish by force !

CHAPTER X

THE ARMY, THE STATE, AND LABOUR

I HAVE argued that in the political State militarism cannot be controlled by the true democratic will, but that when it is trusted it must dominate, and I have now to consider what its effects are upon the industrial State.

I am not to discuss here the industrial cost of conscription—the loss in ineffective and wasted labour, the burden imposed upon the young workmen, and so on—because that has been done elsewhere, and I wish in this study to confine my thoughts to the more political aspects of the problem. I simply note this important consideration in passing.[1]

Jaurès has not much to say about this, but his argument is that the Army, at any rate in France, has no will of its own. It is not something, as it is in Turkey, Greece, or Spain, which plots revolutions and takes an active part in government. In France it is obedient to the civil authority.

[1] Mr. Glasier discusses it in his pamphlet on *Conscription*, published by the Independent Labour Party.

It is a tool. It is something which the democracy can use for its own ends.

We are not very much interested in Cæsarism—the government by the Army—in Great Britain. Our fear is rather that the Army can always be used as a tool. The point which Jaurès made to allay the fears of the French democracy is one which we should make to rouse the suspicions of our people.

The Army is obedient. Universal military training means a nation under the discipline of officers, not a nation under the discipline of its own mind. Hence it is often argued that in a democratic State an Army is no menace. It obeys the rulers, the political chiefs, and therefore follows the popular will. Such is the argument.

This argument only rings the changes on the word " democracy " and makes it bear a meaning which does not belong to it. There is no State of any consequence to-day controlled by the interests of the industrial classes. This statement is not contradicted by the fact that in some nations there is manhood suffrage. The interests which control even democratic nations are those which are well organized, vigilant, and coherent—those which own the Press and the political machinery of the constituencies ; those from whom Ministers are taken ; the families which pay £400 a year to get their sons into the Diplomatic Service. The industrial classes are an influence more or less remote, especially between elections, but are not a steady political authority. Thus the State is less democratic than the nation. Now, the Army is the servant of the State, not of the nation. That is the fundamental fact which we have to bear in mind. If this distinction between State and nation were removed by democratic Governments, international diplomacy would be so altered that armies would be altogether unnecessary. The whole problem would be solved ; it would not have to be settled by compromises and safeguards. It would not exist.

With Jaurès, we object to an Army which has a will of its own and makes rulers and revolutions ; but we also object to his Army which is a tool of the State, because the State uses the Army to support the interests which control the State.

Whilst the distinction between State and nation lasts, the industrial danger of the armed nation is real and pressing. The Army will be used for industrial purposes, especially in times of trade disputes. The best recent case is that of the French railway strike, the story of which is as follows : The French railway employees were conducting an agitation for Trade Union recognition in 1910, and those of the south obtained it ; but it was refused to those of the north, and in October they came out on strike, M. Briand, who came into political prominence as a syndicalist firebrand of the extreme type, had worked his way up the political ladder and was then Premier. He instantly mobilized the Army and put it to running the trains. Thus Jacques left his engine one night as a Trade Unionist and stepped upon it next morning as a soldier under instructions to defeat himself as a Trade Unionist. Some who refused were punished by court-martial as soldiers. The strike was broken. That is a very simple form of industrial conscription which will no doubt be used frequently should the conflict between Labour and Capital in the future become severe and all attempts to solve it by peaceful means be defeated. A nation of conscripts is a nation of potential strike-breakers. Free labour associations under the French methods are unnecessary institutions.

Since the war broke out and conscription was established here, military service has been used to coerce workmen and punish Trade Unionists. Foremen have decided who have to be taken and who left. Men have been compelled to join the Army and have been sent back to work as soldiers. Cases are innumerable. Ministers did not mean it. When they pledged themselves that this would not happen, I do not believe they had any thought of making it happen. The true explanation is that militarism cannot be worked so as not to involve industrial conscription.[1]

[1] These are some interesting facts :—
Mr. Asquith's pledge to Labour deputation on January 12, 1916 : " I cannot imagine anything more monstrous than that

But the more common form of using the military is to overawe the workmen. Great Britain affords the best example of that. When the railway strike broke out here in 1911, the Home Office, under Mr. Winston Churchill, immediately put itself at the head of the military and in turn put the military at the disposal of the railway directors. Troops were put in possession of the lines and were paraded fully armed in front of the men. They were sent

advantage should be taken of this opportunity to introduce a method by which unscrupulous and unpatriotic employers would get additional power over workmen. I am not in favour of compulsion in regard to industrial work. I see no reason for it. I shall absolutely resist it to the last."—*Times*. *Mr. Bonar Law :* "There was no intention whatever in this Bill to introduce in any shape or form industrial conscription."—*Hansard*, p. 317, January 8, 1916.

Such was the intention. This is the experience :—

"Within a month of the passing of the Military Service Act there was a strike at Dundee. . . . What did the employer do ? He did not use the ordinary methods of a dispute and fight it out. . . . He immediately reported these men to the military authorities, and they were called up under the Act."—*J. H. Thomas, M.P.* (*Hansard*, May 16, 1916). "A working party of 102 soldiers was supplied to the Llanelly Steel Company. These men . . . remain in the military service of the Crown, and are under military discipline. They receive no wages, but continue in receipt of their military emoluments."—*Dr. Addison, Ministry of Munitions* (*Hansard*, p. 671, August 7, 1916).

Mr. Robert Smillie, speaking at Edinburgh, stated that he had been informed of a case where a miner had been sent back to work in a mine, and had been told by an officer that he was to go back to a particular mine and stay in that mine, and that any disobedience would result in his being at once sent back to the Army.

to towns that had never asked for them and where their presence was regarded as an insult. Men returning in the dead of the night from negotiations designed to end the trouble found themselves held up by the secret movement of troops on the streets. By the end of the week the country was, in consequence, on the verge of the most serious civil discord. At the time the foreign situation was bad, owing to the difficulties about Morocco, and that restrained the Home Office and the State authorities and peace was brought about. Thus by a mere coincidence the country was undoubtedly saved from serious bloodshed and the workmen from a complete defeat.

The shooting of strikers during riotous disturbances arising out of strikes and lock-outs is still more common. Such shooting is generally ill-timed and the victims are as a rule innocent people. This violence does no good. It neither protects property nor allays passion. It takes place as a rule when local authorities lose their heads. But the military being at the beck and call of magistrates who are generally prejudiced against the workmen, and often interested in the issues of the dispute, is a grave disadvantage to the Unions and provokes men to excesses. The police forces are perfectly competent to deal with any trouble that may arise, especially if the local authorities were compelled to seek the co-operation of the leaders of the strikers to prevent disturbance. This would be far more

effective than bringing files of soldiers with ball
cartridge in front of excited mobs. The military,
however, are really used to end the strike and to
punish for destroyed property, not to keep order.
They are an industrial force, not a police one.

In this way the military—a citizen army with
citizen officers—has been used in Switzerland, in
Australia under a Labour Government, in South
Africa under a Government which apparently had
no sympathy with mine-owners, in France, in
Germany, and in Russia.

An army is always a powerful weapon in the
hands of Governments to destroy the chances of
labour in a hard-fought industrial dispute. It is
never used against capital, for in the nature of things
it cannot be so used. The interest of capital
is not of such a kind as would bring it into
conflict with the military, even when it is in direct
conflict with the law and ought to be in conflict
with the police. A conscript nation puts special
powers in the hands of capital to control labour
and hamper its freedom, and that power has always
been used whenever and wherever occasion has
arisen.

But there is something more than this that has to
be said. No line can be drawn between the camp
and the workshop. An efficient military camp must
have an obedient workshop behind it. Production
of munitions, of food, clothing, and other necessities

is absolutely essential to an army, and an autocratic control of that production is necessary for the nation which leans upon force for its security. When the armies are called up the places of the enlisted men in field, mine, and workshop must be taken at once. This means the training of women during peace. No nation in the future can neglect this, for conscription has been proved by this war to be as necessary as regards tools as it is as regards arms. Function after function of the nation has to submit to be painted khaki, as the nation with increasing completeness organizes itself to defend itself by force. General Skugarevski is perfectly right. The military nations of the future must prepare their workshops for war. Those that are most thorough will train their women by a process of conscription, because the woman worker in the time of war is essential to the State. She is a reserve to be mobilized on the outbreak of war, and her mobilization requires preconcerted plans and preliminary training.

So, just as there is no distinction in actual fact between a policy of armed defence and offence, there is none between military and industrial conscription. The former cannot be worked without calling the latter to its aid.

CHAPTER XI

THE ARMY AND REVOLUTION

THERE are some Socialists and Trade Unionists in this country who advocate a citizen Army of a special kind which they do not hesitate to say they will use if they can for a special purpose. They would train all men in arms; the officers would come from the ranks, or, in any event, commissions would be open to the working classes; barrack discipline would not be rigid and the regimental aspect of militarism would be reduced to a minimum. Their idea is to train citizens in the use of arms and in military drill, organization, and cohesion, and their purpose is to defend the nation if need be against invasion, and to use force also if need be in industrial disputes. One of them is reported to have said, "We want to be able to meet armed force with armed force if the capitalists use it."

That method of social progress has no attractions for me; and the people of influence who are pushing universal military service can afford to smile at such a card up Labour's sleeve. They will take care that if my friend gets his citizen Army he will not get his revolution as well. He will never get that card down his sleeve.

The idea that arms are a badge of liberty and an evidence of power and that they are useful to overawe rulers and secure domestic reform is an old revolutionary one. The armed nation used to appear in every revolutionary programme.[1] But that was before the franchise, which armed intelligent men with something far more powerful than a rifle and more deadly than a sword. " What is the use of liberty if we are not armed to protect it? " is as dead as Queen Anne as a piece of political wisdom. He who cannot use the vote cannot use the rifle, and to try to revive this ancient doctrine is putting the clock back. The armed nation will be the tool of the State. The Socialist who thunders one moment against the existing capitalist State, and demands the next that the nation ought to be armed, may fancy he is speaking with magnificent dash and thoroughness, but in reality he is only demanding that the worker should put his neck more securely into the yoke of capitalism, should impose upon himself a discipline and

[1] Nothing has been written in its favour that is better than Major Cartwright's *Ægis, or the Military Energies of the Constitution* (1804). The argument was appropriate to the time, but one has only to read the book to understand how the conditions of the more revolutionary section of political parties has changed since then.

obedience which stunt the free growth of the democratic spirit of initiative and freedom, and should hand himself over to an organization which, from its very nature, must be controlled by State authorities whom he as a soldier cannot disobey without incurring the direst penalties and punishments.

Revolution in some countries may yet be necessary to open out the road for freedom; but when it is successful it will only bring the workmen of such a country to the position now held by the workers of Great Britain, and at that point they will have to lay aside arms and tout for votes. There may be a lack of romantic heroism about this, but the part of the romantic hero is generally played by the Socialist who talks and poses. It is not real business.

Jaurès does make the point that when officers are drawn from the democracy the control of the Army will not be so completely in the hands of the State authorities. He discusses this very fully, but comes to the conclusion that Socialists and Trade Unionists should accept all the risks and take commissions. They will be able to use their power on behalf of the workers, and the capitalist will find, with them in authority, an Army not so pliable to the will of the State. But that means that the Army will then have a will of its own, and that there will be Army politics. No greater evil can befall the democratic State than this. Cæsarism, even if it be inspired by democratic feelings, is an evil. The supreme power in the democratic State must be civil, and if that be bad it must be reformed or changed politically. The very worst way to remedy such a state of things is to create an Army which will have the power and the will to accept or reject orders from the duly constituted civil authority. The mutinous conspiracy of the Unionist officers at the Curragh Camp was bad, not because it was directed against a decision of Parliament which suited Liberal and Labour opinion, but because it was a conspiracy of officers and an interference of the Army as such in civil affairs. The whole of the Ulster movement is a splendid illustration of the evil which will arise if the Army, however wrong the decisions of Parliament may be, is taught to believe that it holds in its hands the power to thwart Parliament. The inherent objection to military rule is only intensified by the deliberate pursuit of a method of selecting officers which will give some promise that the Army will be used in an enfranchised nation on the side of democracy if democracy should have occasion to quarrel with its civil and representative rulers.

But the selection of officers from the industrial classes is no guarantee that the Army will be democratized. An officer from whatever rank he is drawn is trained in his military job, and the vast majority of such men will take on the tinge of militarism, will look upon politics and the State from militarist angles of vision, and allow their minds to be run into militarist moulds. Experience shows that there is no man more ready than he who has risen from the working class to adapt himself to the habits and point of view of other classes, and in the Army I believe it is true that the officer who has risen from the ranks has adopted to a special degree the mind and discipline of the soldier. The problem of how to make Cabinets representative in all their acts is a political and not a military one, and armed citizens cannot assist to solve it.

The Social Revolution, if made at all, must be made in the workshop and through the ballot-box, by the citizen himself changing his opinions and life, by the workman assuming more industrial power, and by the elector showing more political intelligence in the management of his affairs.

CHAPTER XII

THE GUARANTEE OF PEACE

My argument thus far has been :

1. National defence cannot be confined to defensive precautions, but must become an offensive if it is based upon military force, however that force is officered or constituted;

2. A military organization is a weapon in the hands of the State for industrial purposes, partly because the State is always less democratic than the nation, and partly because industrial warfare must always raise questions of national security and existence;

3. No line can be drawn between the military and the industrial order. The military authority must embrace the workshop because industrial production is necessary to an army. Military conscription must involve industrial conscription ; and

4. After this war, unless there is a complete change in the inspiration and control of international policy, Great Britain will have to accept, in addition to its special obligation to provide the most powerful Navy in Europe, the same military responsibility

as any other continental Power, and that means that conscription will have to be a peace expedient as well as a war necessity.

Two points still remain to be discussed. The first is guarantees of national safety, and, arising from that, the kind of peace which ought now to be striven for.

The Russian General Skugarevski, who gave the interview to which I have already referred, concluded his conversation with some remarkable opinions. When Germany has been subdued, he said, the States of Europe might agree, as has already been proposed at The Hague, to limit armaments. Then he remarked, " An international tribunal must at last acquire power." Finally, he made an important admission. What power? Is power only armed power? He goes on :—

Some people think that this power can be defended only by the armed hand, whilst, since it is impossible to create a kind of international Hague army, the decisions of an international tribunal will be equivalent merely to "scraps of paper." No. The decisions of an international tribunal can rest, first, on the strength of public opinion.

The second foundation-stone of this power may be economic, according to General Skugarevski.

The guarantee of peace is educated public opinion, acting through a State or controlling a Government, and there is no other. Even a threatened economic war is of little consequence. That one

8

nation can punish another by refusing to trade
with it is an idea which breaks down when examined
in the details of its process. It assumes the false
premises of Tariff Reform—viz. that political nations
trade with each other, whereas trade is conducted
only between certain individuals of the nations.
If the economic punishment is meted out in a limited
way, only certain persons and interests suffer, and
these will not be the guilty persons or the offending interests; if it can be carried out to the extent
of a general blockade, nobody but the poor will
suffer for a long time, and interests that are really
national will be untouched until the consequences
of the blockade have spread upwards through
society. The blockade purpose is to cause revolution by the starvation of the helpless ones of a
nation. Whilst the economic war is in operation
all the complicated channels through which international trade runs will have to be explored and
drained of the trade of the offending nation, and
this will not only mean much irritation amongst
the injured interests of the other nations but much
punishment of the people of all countries. The
method is ineffective, inaccurate, and clumsy. On
paper, it is a threat ; in reality, it is an impossibility.

Let us concentrate our attention upon the real
facts.

The only way to provide for national security
is to remove the fears and arbitrate upon the mis-

understandings and rivalries which grow up into conflicts when armies are available and the possession of force is an inducement to rulers to be unbending. The problem, if apparently difficult to solve, is easy to state. It is this :—

No people wants to fight any other people. Public opinion in times of peace is always against war; it becomes warlike only when roused by the bugles of war, blowing from Foreign Offices, Ministries of War, and through newspapers. How are national disputes to be settled by the people before their passions are aroused? I have said that this is apparently difficult, but in reality the ease with which it can be done is the great obstacle to doing it. Foreign affairs in some mysterious way have been withdrawn from the light of the world. They are transacted in rooms with blinds drawn, with backstairs entrances and secret doors and waiting chambers. Upon them are employed spies, suborned agents, ambassadors whose business it is to cheat, and *finesse*. The whole corrupting system should be swept away. It stands like a dirty old slum area, full of vermin and disease, in the midst of a district cleared and improved. It belongs to the kind of evil which exists by leaning upon a similar evil which, in turn, exists by leaning upon it. Few seem to see that a kick at any of the supports will bring the whole offensive fabric down.

Supposing Mr. Asquith had informed both

Germany, and ourselves in 1912 that the two countries had failed to come to an understanding, instead of assuring us that we were on terms of the most complete agreement, how different events would have been ! Supposing it had been the habit of people to regard foreign relations as within the scope of democratic control, and our rulers had been afraid to commit the country's honour without sanction, again, how different things would have been ! Even assuming that the German authorities were then bent on war, an open diplomacy on our part would have prevented the German people from being hoodwinked, would have rendered the rush to arms at the end of July 1914 impossible, and would have defeated the policy of the Governments to begin the war by persuading all their peoples that each was fighting a defensive battle. Or supposing I am too pacifically optimist and nothing could have prevented war, an honest statement of our dangers and an unmistakable proof that they, were real would have led to preparation (say in food and other supplies) adequate to the risk.

I do not make the mistake of assuming that open diplomacy will remove the *causes* of war; I do say, that it will enable these causes to dissipate themselves without an explosion. Secret diplomacy acts upon national rivalry as a confining chamber acts upon a high explosive. In the open the high explosive burns; in a confined place it explodes.

Capitalist rivalries, the spirit which animated our Tariff Reform campaigns, the need of national expansion, such as both Russia and Germany feel, will provide plenty of causes for future wars, but an open diplomacy will prevent these causes from generating disruptive force. The people and reasonableness will settle them as they arise.

There is no other guarantee of peace and national security. No army can give it; no treaty under existing conditions can give it. It can only be given by the people themselves insisting upon knowing to what their rulers are committing them and what game their diplomatists are playing and upon taking responsibility upon themselves. Everybody will not do this. Heaven help us if that were necessary ! But many agencies of goodwill and intelligent political thought and action will do so, and that will suffice.

The argument I have been stating in this chapter was always present in Jaurès' mind when considering how far his military views were applicable to Great Britain. He believed, as I have already, said, that we could do better than create a citizen force for national defence. In the English translation of his book appears the following significant pronouncement :— [1]

There are two courses open to England as regards her foreign and colonial policy. By following the lines so ably laid down

[1] *Democracy and Military Service*, pp. 124-5.

by the advocates of peace—the Socialists, the Labour Party, the best and most courageous members of the Radical Party—England can play a decisive part in inducing Europe and the world at large to adopt a policy of peace. In that case she will grant far-reaching concessions—both political and social—to Egypt and to India, and will thus avert the revolts with which she is threatened. She will accept, she will herself propose, the abolition of the right to seize private property at sea ; and by thus weakening the power of naval war, she will do away with all danger of war being brought about by the economic rivalry between herself and Germany. By adopting the principle of arbitration as applicable to all international disputes, she will open up the way to progressive reduction of armaments. By such measures the economic forces both of England and of other countries will be enabled to follow their natural course, and the law of nations will easily be able so to extend its jurisdiction as to prevent industrial and mercantile rivalry from leading to fraud or violence.

England may, on the other hand, refuse to follow this wise and beneficent policy. And in that case the half-hearted measures elaborated by Mr. Haldane for the purpose of national defence will certainly not enable her to face the dangers which she foresees in the future—national and religious uprisings in Egypt and in India, and the dreaded conflict with Germany, whose naval force, growing day by day, threatens the coasts and, at any rate, the imagination of England.

Mr. Haldane's Territorial organization is one of those ingenious compromises which English statesmanship excels in creating. But it will probably not be able in the long run to withstand the varied attacks to which its complexity exposes it. If ever the danger of a world-wide war comes home to the masses of the English nation, the territorial system as it exists will probably be swamped.

The war has rendered some of the phrases in the above extract old, but the idea and argument behind them are as sound now as when they were published in 1910.

Should any one urge that we must arm because
other people are arming and defend because other
people are threatening, my reply is : It is not our
business to content ourselves with allowing other
people to take the initiative, and to consider ourselves wise in merely countering their moves; we
ought to have a clearly mapped out policy to secure
peace, and we ought to pursue it; if for the time
being we are driven to do something that is not
altogether in accord with it, we should recognize
that we run great risks in doing so.   But chiefly
my reply is that this game of following an evil
lead is one of life and death to the nations, because
it is an endless game.   The resort to militarism
provided the conditions which make militarism
necessary—more militarism and still more militarism,
more danger and still more danger.   The " practical " man whose vision is limited by his existing
conditions and whose mind is satisfied by reflecting
that disarmament is at present unpractical is, as
usual, not practical at all.   He is a passive dreamer.
Arms have been proved by history to be the most
unpractical of all expedients to secure either peace
or justice.   To go on trusting to old broken reeds
is foolishness, not wisdom.   By an effort of will
we must become civilized men.   Nothing else will
be of any use.   We are like a squirrel in a revolving
cage; the faster we run, the faster we have to
run.   One day the nations will have the courage

and the wisdom to step out. The instant they do so they will find themselves in a peaceful world.

In every nation after this war there will be a specially keen interest in the causes and effects of militarism, and every nation will be willing to consider the subject of peace. Some nations will be dominated by the military spirit, perhaps because they are sulky and have scores to wipe off, perhaps because they are afraid. But in every nation there will be a clear-sighted peace party. If these parties, acting internationally, are not strong enough to hold militarism in absolute check and to impose upon it an increasing control, they must subordinate many differences in their own domestic politics in order to strengthen international democratic organizations. The great political issues of this war will be fought out after the war ends, not by it, nor during it. A strong united effort will be required in which enlightened opinion in the various nations must be in the very closest communion, must act both officially and unofficially on arranged plans in the separate States, must devise and support policies to strengthen the pacific movements in each country, and must create both a national and international political organization which in every country will act in unity. The days of peace picnics and polite and meaningless speeches are over. They have been empty. Energy that is sleepless and a policy which is pursued from day to day and with complete detail, watching every move in the diplomatic game and with a thoroughly efficient Intelligence Department and Parliamentary policy, are now required if the men who have died for us are not to have died in vain.

CHAPTER XIII

THE POLITICS OF PEACE

MEANWHILE we must consider the politics of peace, for peace is a political and not a military problem. Amongst the truths that history teaches with a conclusiveness which cannot be questioned is that a peace made by military victors in the spirit of military victors is no peace at all. To-day we are deluded by such catch-penny phrases as " a premature peace," " no patched-up peace," and so on. They are quite meaningless and very delusive. They imply the doctrine, which I have said history proves to be wrong and mischievous, that war can make peace. You can punish a nation by war, you can devastate it, you can rob it of its territory and impose an indemnity to cripple it in the future, but you cannot in this way make peace. Never can any nation have a more complete victory over another than Germany had over France when the Franco-German War ended, and never was peace more patently " patched-up " or more clearly vitiated by the qualities of inconclusiveness than the Peace of

Frankfurt in May 1871. France and Germany lived
in a state of armed truce from 1871 to 1914, and
the whole of Europe knew it.   The shadow, the
fears, the disturbance of the imminent war perturbed
Europe throughout the whole generation ; it determined European diplomacy ;   it defeated every
attempt to arrive at settled agreement ; it created
the Alliance of the Central Powers and the Entente
between the surrounding nations ; finally, it merged
itself in the causes of this war.

The blindness of a people at war believing that
absolute military victory is the only way to peace
characterizes all wars.   It is now more than an
arguable proposition that we could have made a
better peace in 1800 than we did fifteen years
later.   The Treaty of Paris which ended the
Crimean War in 1856 was considered by Queen
Victoria as "rather premature" and was opposed
by Palmerston.   As a matter of fact, it could have
been secured in 1855.   Mr. J. A. Farrer, writing
in the *Manchester Guardian*, says, after a survey
of the seven great wars of the last two centuries to
which this country has been a party :—

When one thinks of the countless millions of lives that have
been sacrificed in these former wars by their needless prolonga-
tion, for some insignificant aim, or for some party purpose of
the time, one is inclined to execrate the memory of those who,
in their rejection of premature peaces, effected belated ones
which added so unnecessarily to the world's sufferings.   It is not
a premature peace that we have to fear so much as a belated
one ; for the balance of history is on the side of those who in

former wars favoured what seemed a premature peace, not on the side of those who prolonged those wars for no result that justified their continuance.

When a war breaks out it drives with its terrible force the peoples of all the belligerent nations into what is called the patriotic camp. They all believe they are right. Then some measure of calm comes. The first pain of death and suffering is sobering. They all feel hatred of the slaughter and are disturbed by the privations. That also begins to pass, however. People get accustomed to death both at home and on the field, and suffering becomes habitual. By that time the military pressure has begun to show itself, and through the mists we can see how the battle sways and which side is likely to be beaten. The victor is unwilling to stay his hand ; the conquered fights to remove disgrace. Then the military end comes. The cannons can fire no more, and the vanquished nation, sullen, angry, and resentful, like poor, unhappy Queen Mary, nurses its grievance in its heart and begins to study revenge. Civilization and the pacific purposes of the peoples have been defeated. Militarism, beaten on the field, retires into the hearts of the people as into a sanctuary. That is the course of all national wars, and the failure of all statesmen hitherto is that they have allowed that full course to be run.

It seems absurd, but it is true, that the future peace depends, not on the victor but on the vanquished. It is not the amount of military success but that of military defeat which determines whether the nations are to settle down. It is because this is true that victors so often make a mess of things and undo the military results of war by the political consequences. By assuming that the victors can settle things, we forget that the essential problem is to get the vanquished to accept things.

A simple truth recognized by all military writers, but turned by them to imperfect use, is always obscured in the minds of people during a war. It is that war is an incident in political policy, like a spurt in the course of a race.[1] When it is over, the political policy goes on again, and the value of the war is determined by whether it has aided or hindered the policy. This truth must be hammered at and hammered at. If this war does not end militarism and the menace of force, the object of the British people in accepting it will have been betrayed.

So I return to the political question. When, in that evolution of popular feeling during a war, has war reached its maximum political effect? Evidently somewhere about the middle, just at the time when the crowds are being urged to shout that they will have no inconclusive peace.

---

[1] " In one word, the art of war in its highest point of view is policy. War is only a part of political intercourse, therefore by no means an independent thing in itself."—CLAUSEWITZ.

Students of Clausewitz will remember that in a finely impressive passage in his book *On War,* he insists that the military leaders should always keep before them the art of forcing the people of the enemy nation into a frame of mind which induces them to submit. That pregnant idea is much wider in its common sense than Clausewitz saw. It means that the statesmen as well as the generals of the belligerent nations should study the minds of their enemies, for a willingness to submit arises, not from the fear and the sacrifice of war but from mental and moral opinions as well. This justifies—nay, indeed it necessitates—the demand of such bodies as the Union of Democratic Control that statesmen should make their intentions clear, not only in order that the peoples at war should understand what they are fighting for and what they are fighting against, but also that the statesmen themselves may have the ends they think the war is to serve definitely, before them, and so prevent the war from entering upon a stage when every new military success only drives the political goal farther and farther off. If the rulers who conduct wars really mean to establish peace permanently in the end, war and diplomacy together must be inspired by the Clausewitz idea, and the object of waging war must be to produce in the minds of the peoples such attitudes as incline them to accept peace. A war which ends in unwilling submission, or which leaves as an inheritance

fresh causes of war, is not ended at all.   For the
" end " of a war is not military victory but peace.
The military mind assumes, as a matter of fact, that
war can never end, but the civil mind makes no
such assumption.   That is why the military mind
thinks only of " absolute " victory in terms of military success, whereas the civil mind ought to think
of it in terms of political success.   To-day we are
sacrificing political success and ultimate peace to
military success.   For it is clear that the political
climax does not coincide with the military climax,
the former coming when weariness without resent-
ment is at its maximum, the latter when defeat is
absolute and humiliation is deepest.

From this point of view the Army is an instrument in the hands of the men responsible for political
policy, and that is why we must apply a maxim of
the militarists themselves in a wider and truer way
than they apply it.   Clausewitz wrote that " the first,
the grandest, and most decisive act of judgment
which the statesman and general exercises " is to
understand precisely what the object of war is, and
not " wish to make of it something which, by the
nature of its relations, it is impossible for it to be."
The statesman of any capacity and judgment ought
to know when the war has secured him his political
object, and then immediately put his political forces
into action and so win his purpose.   That is exactly
what our statesmen never do and what the men at

present at the head of affairs are declining to do. Be they Conservative or Liberal, militarist Labour or Socialist, they belong to the old order who see in the triumph and the support of force the conditions of peace. They are where the Congress of Vienna and the Conferences of Paris and Frankfurt were. And yet upon the ending of this war politically, and upon that alone, depends the future peace of Europe.

Let us assume that the problem to-day is Germany, and that it centres round the question whether the German military mind is to dominate the policy of that country, and so maintain in Europe a sense of insecurity that has to be temporarily allayed by armaments. How is Europe to get guarantees against this? No sane man would suggest that the Government of Germany can be controlled by any combination of Powers in occupation of Berlin. Sooner or later we have to trust ourselves and Europe to the will and policy of a self-governing Germany. When the best and the worst have been done, Germany will still have it in her power to stir up strife and fear or accept peace. How will military operations affect that will and policy? If Germany is left in the frame of mind in which France was in 1871, obviously the effect upon Europe will be bad. But if Germany is not to be left where France was, equally obviously we must show our trust in her self-governing capacity at the earliest practicable time. To force the popular will of Germany into the arms of militarism is to defeat the very purpose for which we engaged in the war. To end this war with the peoples not on speaking terms is to sacrifice for no gain the thousands of our men left to sleep in Belgium and France, because such an end would not only give militarism a new lease of power but would increase its grip on the throat of civilization.

I believe that the people of Germany now, if released from the strain of the war and the necessity of presenting a united front to the enemy, would end the dominance of militarism, would remove its menace from Europe, and would enter into the co-operation of States which will have to be established if Europe is to be saved from destruction, and I further believe they will be less inclined to that after another year of war. Writing thus, I am no pro-German. I am a pro-European. To me Germany is a problem just as capitalism is a problem, and unless that problem is faced in an atmosphere of scientific rationality it will never be solved at all. Atrocities and brutalities are not only the means by which militarism fights, but those by which it perpetuates itself. They rouse, quite rightly, whirl-winds of moral indignation, and, alas ! under these whirlwinds reason is uprooted. How often do we find in life that a man whose cause is just and whose

9

indignation is altogether worthy is swept to ruin and ineffectiveness by the fury of his moral indignation overwhelming his rational judgment ! Our lunatic asylums, and the wildernesses where our Ishmaels are, are full of such wrecks of good but injured men. From the people gush bountiful springs of pure feeling, but these springs water the weedy fields cultivated by their rulers. I want the crimes committed by Germans punished ; if it can be proved that crimes have been committed against Germany, I want them punished too. If we could get the various peoples into that frame of mind we could have peace, but only in that way.

As to programmes,[1] I do not believe they present much difficulty provided they are considered by the peoples themselves. The restoration of Belgium, the rehabilitation of France, the settlement of the Balkans, the re-establishment of a Polish autonomy, outlets for Germany—these and kindred questions are so agreed upon really in the hearts of the people that no Conference representative of the people could fail to settle them, or could quarrel about the principles upon which they ought to be settled— the recognition of nationality and self-government, the inviolability of properly sanctioned treaties, the

---

[1] I do not consider these in detail, but content myself with referring my readers to such books as *Towards a Lasting Settlement*, by C. R. Buxton and others. George Allen & Unwin, 2s. 6d. net.

desirability of arbitration, the convenience of a Council of the nations.

The danger is that all these questions will be approached when the time comes by men who will assume the possibility of further wars, men who will have enmity brooding in their hearts and who will be in a position to play with nations as their stakes, by men who have not freed themselves from a dependence upon militarism as the only guarantee of national security.

Unless the old order of diplomacy and international policy is swept off the stage by the fury of this war, democracy and militarism will be left at hand-grips upon it and Europe will be doomed to the curse of an armed truce. We have suffered much these past two years. A whole generation of men has been obliterated. National wealth, so much needed to enrich the starved lives of our people, has been wasted. A burden of debt unsurpassed in the history of mankind has been accumulated. Problems of terrible import in the State and the workshop have been created. Is this all to go for naught? Is it " Ichabod " that we are writing on the gateways of the future? Is it " Failure " that the next generation will have to carve on the widely scattered graves of this?

These views may for the moment be unpopular. But they are Truth. They are gathered from the waysides of the past. From them, and from them alone, can we build worthy and abiding monuments upon the graves of the men who have fallen, and to build these monuments no sacrifice imposed upon us by the bitter passions of the moment is too great for us cheerfully to bear.

GEORGE ALLEN & UNWIN LTD., 40 RUSKIN HOUSE, MUSEUM STREET, LONDON, W.C 1

After - War Problems

Edited by William Harbutt Dawson

Demy 8vo.   *7s. 6d. net.*   *Postage 6d.*

This important volume is intended to state some of the more urgent national problems which will need to be faced after the War, and to offer a practicable Programme of Reconstruction. The chapters have all been written by specialists deeply concerned in the subjects with which they deal, as will be seen from the following synopsis :—

IMPERIAL FEDERATION.
By the late EARL OF CROMER.

THE STATE AND THE CITIZEN.
By BISHOP WELLDON.

NATIONAL EDUCATION.
By VISCOUNT HALDANE.

THE ORGANIZATION OF NATIONAL RESOURCES. By the RT. HON. SIR J. COMPTON RICKETT, M.P.

RELATIONS BETWEEN CAPITAL AND LABOUR. (1. LABOUR.) By GEO. H. ROBERTS, J.P., M.P.

RELATIONS BETWEEN CAPITAL AND LABOUR. (2. CAPITAL.) By SIR BENJAMIN C. BROWNE.

THE REHABILITATION OF RURAL LIFE. By the BISHOP OF EXETER.

NATIONAL HEALTH.
By JAMES KERR, M.A., M.D., D.P.H.

UNSOLVED PROBLEMS OF THE ENGLISH POOR LAW. By SIR WM. CHANCE, Bart., M.A.

THE CULTIVATION OF PATRIOTISM
By the EARL OF MEATH.

THE ALIEN QUESTION.
By SIR H. H. JOHNSTON.

THE STATE AND INDUSTRY.
By Dr. W. GARNETT.

THE STATE IN RELATION TO LABOUR. By PROF. S. J. CHAPMAN.

POSITION OF WOMEN IN ECONOMIC LIFE. By MRS. FAWCETT.

THE LAND QUESTION.
By W. JOYNSON HICKS, M.P.

HOUSING AFTER THE WAR.
By HENRY R. ALDRIDGE.

THE CARE OF CHILD LIFE.
By MARGARET MCMILLAN.

NATIONAL THRIFT.
By ARTHUR SHERWELL, M.P.

NATIONAL TAXATION AFTER THE WAR. By PROF. ALFRED MARSHALL.

The Choice Before Us

By G. LOWES DICKINSON

Demy 8vo.   *7s. 6d. net.*   *Postage 6d.*

This book describes briefly the prospect before the world, if the armed international anarchy is to continue, and to be extended and exasperated, after the war. It analyses and discusses the presuppositions which underlie Militarism. And having argued both that international war as it will be conducted in the future implies the ruin of civilization, and that it is not "inevitable," sketches the kind of reorganization that is both possible and essential if war is not to destroy mankind.

LONDON : GEORGE ALLEN & UNWIN LIMITED

A Bulwark against Germany

The Fight of the Slovenes, the Western Branch of the Jugoslavs, for National Existence

By BOGUMIL VOSNJAK

Late Lecturer of the University of Zagreb (Croatia).

TRANSLATED BY FANNY S. COPELAND

Crown 8vo.   *4s. 6d. net.*   *Postage 5d.*

After the dismemberment of the Habsburg Empire the union of the Jugoslav nation—the Serbs, Croats, and Slovenes—in one State will be one of the most important features of future Europe. From the beginning of the Middle Ages down to the present great war the western-most branch of this nation, the Slovenes, have waged a brave struggle against German imperialism. The "Bulwark" explains ¦the historical, political, social, and economical evolution of the Slovenes, who will be a strong factor in the building up of the great Serbia or Jugoslavia of to-morrow.

A Dying Empire

By BOGUMIL VOSNJAK

WITH A PREFACE BY T. P. O'CONNOR, M.P.

Crown 8vo.   *4s. 6d. net.*   *Postage 5d.*

In this account of the Dying Empire of Austria the author has tried to describe the sociological factors in the breakdown of the Hapsburg Empire, and to show that in the fabric of a "Central Europe" is closely woven the idea of a predominating Pan-Germanism. Either Germany must stretch from Hamburg to Trieste and Salonika, or Austria-Hungary must be dismembered. There is no alternative.

Practical Pacifism and its Adversaries : "Is it Peace, Jehu ?"

By DR. SEVERIN NORDENTOFT

WITH AN INTRODUCTION BY G. K. CHESTERTON

Crown 8vo.   *4s. 6d. net.*   *Postage 5d.*

In addition to making definite suggestions as to the lines on which the Peace Movement should go to work after the war—suggestions which are both obvious and practical—the book contains a reprint of a pamphlet written by an upper-class native of Schleswig, with footnote criticisms by a Prussian scholar of unbiassed views, which renders very sensational and personal testimony to the terrible discontent and bitter rage which a conquered nation feels in its humiliating position of subjection—thus proving beyond all doubt that the chief obstacle that the Peace Movement has to face is this unnatural denial to the conquered people of the Rights of Peace.

LONDON: GEORGE ALLEN & UNWIN LIMITED

The Menace of Peace

By GEORGE D. HERRON

Crown 8vo. 2*s.* 6*d. net.* *Postage* 4*d.*

The purpose of " The Menace of Peace " is to show that the war is but the outward expression of a human conflict that is spiritual, and the issue of which will decide destiny for long centuries to come. The world is at the cross-roads of history, and is there summoned to decide between the democratic principle represented, however unconsciously, by the Allies, and the autocratic principle, consciously represented by the Central Powers. The war, in its last analysis, is between elemental earth-forces incarnated in Germany and the Christ principle which has slowly and even doubtfully gained recognition in the democratic countries. For the war to close, and the world not know what it has been fighting about, would be the supreme catastrophe of history. A compromise between the contending belligerents would be a betrayal of the peoples of every nation, and would issue in universal mental and moral confusion, and the millions who have died would have died in vain. The supreme opportunity of man would have proven itself greater than man.

The United States and the War

By GILBERT VIVIAN SELDES

Crown 8vo. 2*s.* 6*d. net.* *Postage* 4*d.*

" The United States and the War " is an explanation of what the United States has done and has not done since August 1914. The explanation is found, not in the political efforts of individuals, but in the traditions and social ideals of the American people themselves. On the same basis the book discusses the possible relations of the United States with the liberal nations of Europe. The author is an American journalist now living in England.

The Present Position and Power of the Press

By HILAIRE BELLOC

Crown 8vo. 2*s.* 6*d. net.* *Postage* 5*d.*

The purpose of this essay is to discuss the evils of the great modern Capitalist Press, its function in vitiating and misinforming opinion, and in putting power into ignoble hands ; its correction by the formation of small independent organs, and their probably increasing effect.

LONDON : GEORGE ALLEN & UNWIN LIMITED

Home Truths about the War

BY THE REV. HUGH B. CHAPMAN, Chaplain of the Savoy

Crown 8vo.   *2s. 6d. net.   Postage 4d.*

An effort to arrive at the psychology of the war so far as it affects ordinary people, and to assert with humour, but without bitterness, truths to which many are longing to give expression. The object of the writer is to insist on the fact that at this moment the combination of patriotism and piety is the one lesson of the war.

Economic Conditions
1815 and 1914

Crown 8vo.   BY H. R. HODGES, B.Sc. (Econ.)   *2s. 6d. net·*

A book of facts concerning a century's progress in the material welfare of the people of England, comparing their economic position and power, occupations and remuneration at the end of one great European war and the outbreak of a greater.

The book, with its interesting tables and diagrams, gives a clear picture of the improvement, and it will also refresh the memories of the conditions and outlook of the people in the last days of peace.

The American League to Enforce Peace

BY C. R. ASHBEE

WITH AN INTRODUCTION BY G. LOWES DICKINSON

Crown 8vo.   *2s. 6d. net.   Postage 5d.*

The American League to Enforce Peace, a study of whose objects by Mr. C. R. Ashbee we publish, may turn out to be one of the great landmarks of the war. It will sever the United States from their traditional policy, and bring them into a new comity of nations. The American challenge is to every democracy in Europe, and it was significant that the League was inaugurated in May 1915 in Independence Hall, the historic home of the signing of the Declaration of Independence. Mr. Ashbee, who, with one exception, was the only Englishman present at the League's inauguration, goes into the question of its policy and the *force* that underlies it (it is no peace campaign). He had occasion, in his year's study of American conditions, to come into personal contact with most of the active workers of the League and the statesmen who have committed themselves to its platform. His book will give the average Englishman a new idea of what Americans are thinking.

LONDON: GEORGE ALLEN AND UNWIN LIMITED